Classic Knitted
VESTS

16 Styles for Men and Women

Nancie M. Wiseman

Martingale®
& C O M P A N Y

Classic Knitted Vests:
16 Styles for Men and Women

© 2003 Nancie M. Wiseman

Martingale & Company®
20205 144th Avenue NE
Woodinville, WA 98072-8478
www.martingale-pub.com

Mission Statement

Dedicated to providing quality products and service to inspire creativity.

Printed in China

08 07 06 05 04 03   8 7 6 5 4 3 2 1

Library of Congress Cataloging-in-Publication Data

Wiseman, Nancie M.
    Classic knitted vests : 16 styles for men and women /
Nancie M. Wiseman.
        p. cm.
    ISBN 1-56477-472-4
    1. Knitting—Patterns.   2. Vests.   I. Title.
    TT835.W56 2003
    746.43'20432—dc21   2003008957

Credits

President: Nancy J. Martin

CEO: Daniel J. Martin

Publisher: Jane Hamada

Editorial Director: Mary V. Green

Managing Editor: Tina Cook

Technical Editor: Ursula Reikes

Copy Editor: Karen Koll

Design Director: Stan Green

Illustrator: Robin Strobel

Cover and Text Designer:
    Stan Green

Fashion Photographer: John Hamel

Photographer's Assistant: Troy Schnyder

Fashion Stylist: Susan Huxley

Hair and Makeup: Colleen Kobrick

Studio Photographer: Brent Kane

Photographed on location on the campus of Muhlenberg College, Allentown, PA, with special thanks to Mike Bruckner, Glen Gerchman, and Amy Williams.

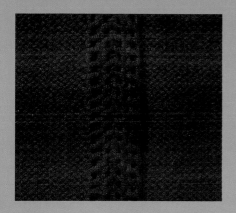  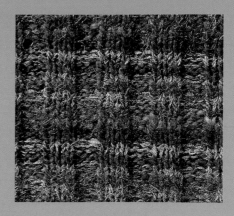

Dedication

This book is dedicated once again to all of you knitters that purchase and love books on knitting. Every effort has been made to make this book a resource for information as well as a source for vest patterns that fit everyone. I hope you enjoy reading the book as much as I loved writing it.

Finishing a book is always bittersweet for me. I work for hours and hours that lead into months and months, and when it's finished it's always hard to let it go. But when the finished book arrives in the mail, the hard work and struggle to get everything in perfect order are soon forgotten. I now turn it over to you, with pleasure.

Acknowledgments

I'd like to mention my husband, Bill, always first on the list. He does everything for me, and I mean everything. Cooks, cleans, shops, and most of all keeps his sense of humor when mine may be gone for one reason or another. He knows I love him, and now you do too. Thank you for moving to Whidbey Island, and thank you for remaining my best friend.

Many thanks to Ursula Reikes, my editor and friend. What a joy to be able to work with you until we get each detail of a book just right. And to everyone at Martingale and Company who makes this work so meaningful and fun. Every one of you is so talented and wonderful to work with. Thank you for making each book you publish special for the author and the consumer. You are a terrific team.

Nancie

Table of Contents

INTRODUCTION
➛ 6

TECHNIQUES AND TIPS
➛ 7

   Short-Row Shaping
for Shoulders ➛ 7

   3-Needle Bind Off ➛ 8

   Substituting Yarns ➛ 9

   Pattern Tips
and Tricks ➛ 10

   Knitting
Abbreviations ➛ 11

MULTI-SIZE VEST FOR
MEN AND WOMEN
➛ 13

FRIDAY HARBOR
➛ 31

SAN FRANCISCO
➛ 35

CHICAGO
➛ 39

COLUMBUS
➛ 43

DALLAS
➛ 47

ANCHORAGE
➛ 53

PUGET SOUND
➛ 57

ATLANTA
➛ 61

PORTLAND
⤳ 65

SAN DIEGO
⤳ 69

WHIDBEY ISLAND
⤳ 73

PHILADELPHIA
⤳ 77

LEXINGTON
⤳ 81

OLYMPIC PENINSULA
⤳ 87

RESOURCES
⤳ 92

BIBLIOGRAPHY
⤳ 93

ABOUT THE AUTHOR
⤳ 95

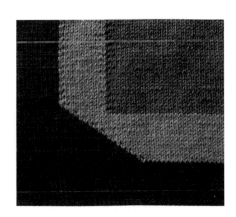

Introduction

I LOVE VESTS! *They are easy to wear, fun to knit, and can be worn anywhere— to the office, outdoors, in the house, out to tea, or to formal gatherings—and in any season. When I'm traveling and teaching, I'm always a little cold, so a vest is terrific for me and leaves my arms free for writing on whiteboards or helping students. Vests are perfect for everybody to wear every day for any activity, and they are perfect for both men and women, no matter what their size.*

In this book you will find that all of the vests range in sizes from small to extra large, and many of them are for both men and women. The yarns used are widely available and the prices vary from modest to mid-range. You'll find a vest for everyone here, and you won't be able to make just one.

In the Multi-Sized Vest for Men and Women, you'll find directions for cardigan and pullover vests in five sizes and in four weights of yarn. There are four borders that can be interchanged for any of the patterns. The four vests shown on pages 12 and 13 illustrate the four weights of yarn and the different borders for both cardigans and pullovers. You'll find that these patterns have so much versatility and so many options that you can make a vest that will fit anyone in any style.

In these vests, you'll find basic stitch patterns like garter stitch, stockinette stitch, reverse stockinette stitch, as well as lace and slip-stitch patterns. There are V-neck pullovers, as well as cardigans with buttons, clasps, and a zipper. Special techniques that refer to a specific vest are given in the vest pattern. For instance, if the vest has a special buttonhole, the "how-to" for that buttonhole will be included in the pattern where it is used.

General techniques, like short-row shaping and 3-needle bind off, that apply to many of the vests are given in the "Techniques and Tips" section. Refer back to these techniques, if needed, when you are instructed to use them in the patterns.

You'll notice that all of the vests are named for a city or an area. A lot of my knitting takes place on airplanes, in cars, and in hotel rooms because of my teaching schedule. I've named the vests for the place where I was teaching when I was working on the vest, where I bought the yarn, where I got the idea, or for the scenery that inspired me. This book is like a diary of my travels for the year 2002. Of course, this idea came to me when I was on an airplane the fall of 2002, while I was coming home from teaching in Michigan.

The variety of designs, as well as the wide range of sizes, will help you find the perfect vests for you to knit for yourself or someone near and dear. I've tried to give you lots of options. I hope you'll find just the vest you're looking for in this book.

Techniques and Tips

T O GET STARTED, *we'll review the techniques for short-row shaping and 3-needle bind off. You'll also find a section on substituting yarns and choosing your size, plus a list of abbreviations and a special section on tips and tricks for working with these patterns.*

Short-Row Shaping for Shoulders

Many of the patterns in this book use short-row shaping for the shoulders. This technique allows you to use 3-needle bind off to create a smooth seam.

Knit-Side Short Rows

These short rows are done on the right side, and on the right front and left back shoulders. Follow the example below using the first size listed to understand the process. We know it is knit-side short rows being worked, because the first direction given is to knit a certain number of stitches.

The directions given in the pattern would instruct you to work the short-row shaping in this manner:

Next row (RS): Knit or work in patt for 9 (10, 12, 12, 14) sts, W and T, work back in pattern. K4 (5, 6, 6, 7), W and T, work back in patt. Work one more row to retrieve wraps.

This translates to: On the next right-side row, knit 9 stitches (for the small size) and then work a wrap and turn (W and T) as follows: *Slip the first stitch on the left needle over to the right needle as if to purl. Move the yarn toward you between the stitches on the knitting needles. Move the first stitch on the right knitting needle (the one you moved originally) over to the left needle as if to purl. Move the yarn between the stitches on the two knitting needles, back to the opposite side*. Turn the work, and purl across the 9 stitches you just knit. Now, knit 4 stitches and work from * to * above. Turn the work and purl the 4 stitches you just knit.

Work one last row to retrieve or "knit up" the "wraps" you placed around the stitches as follows: (They look like purl bumps on the right side of the work.) Knit to the first stitch that is wrapped, insert the right knitting needle **under** the wrap, and knit it together with the stitch it is wrapped around.

Repeat for each wrapped stitch across the row. In this example you would have one more wrap to retrieve. Finish the row. Place stitches on a holder or bind off as directed in the pattern.

Slip stitch as if to purl. Move yarn toward you and slip stitch back to left needle.

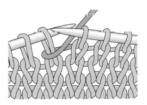

Move yarn to the opposite side. Turn.

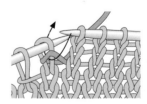

On the final row, knit bar (wrap) and stitch together.

Purl-Side Short Rows

These short rows are done on the wrong side, and on left front and right back shoulders. The matching purl or wrong side short rows from the same pattern would direct you to work the following:

Next row (WS): Purl or work in patt for 9 (10, 12, 12, 14) sts, W and T, work back in pattern. Work 4 (5, 6, 6, 7) sts in patt, W and T, work back. Work one more row to retrieve wraps.

This translates to: On the next wrong-side row, purl 9 stitches and then work a wrap and turn (W and T) as follows: *Slip the first stitch on the left needle over to the right needle as if to purl. Move the yarn away from you between the stitches on the knitting needles. Move the first stitch on the right knitting needle (the one you moved originally) over to the left needle as if to purl. Move the yarn between the stitches on the two knitting needles, back to the opposite side*. Turn the work and knit across the 9 stitches you just purled. Now, purl 4 stitches and work from * to * above. Turn the work and knit the 4 stitches you just purled.

Work one last row to retrieve the "wraps" you placed around the stitches as follows: (They will also look like purl bumps on the right side of the work.) Purl to the first stitch that is wrapped, insert the right knitting needle under the wrap on the right side and purl it together with the stitch it is wrapped around. Repeat for

each wrapped stitch across the row. In this example you would have one more wrap to retrieve. Finish the row. Place stitches on a holder or bind off as directed in the pattern.

Slip stitch as if to purl. Move yarn away from you, slip stitch back to left needle.

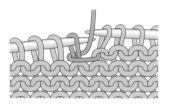

Move yarn to the opposite side. Turn.

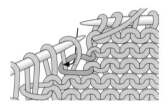

On final row, purl bar (wrap) and stitch together.

In the Multi-Size Vest for Men and Women the pattern is slightly different and will direct you as follows:

Work first short row 7 (8, 8, 8, 9) sts from armhole edge.

Work second short row 6 (6, 8, 8, 9) sts from previous short row.

Work one final row to retrieve wraps.

Using the first size as an example, you would work until there are 7 stitches remaining on the left needle from the armhole edge. Wrap and turn and work

back. You would then work to 6 stitches from the previous wrap and turn, wrap and turn and work back. Work 1 more row to retrieve wraps.

These are more generic directions than given in the first example and will apply to knit-side or purl-side short rows. You will need to be careful and work the short row in the correct manner for the specific shoulder. If you remember to *work knit-side short rows for the right front or the left back shoulder, and purl-side short rows for the left front and right back shoulder,* you won't go wrong.

3-Needle Bind Off

Place shoulder stitches on knitting needles, so that right sides are facing and needle tips are pointing in the same direction. If you use double-pointed or circular needles, there will be a tip at each end, so it doesn't matter which way you put the needles in. With the right sides together, and needle tips toward the right, *knit together 1 stitch from the front needle and 1 stitch from the back needle*. Repeat from * to * once, giving you 2 stitches on the right needle. Bind off loosely. Repeat from * to * once, there are 2 stitches on the right needle again. Bind off loosely. Continue in this manner until all of the stitches are knit together and bound off. Cut yarn, finish off by pulling the cut yarn through the last loop on the needle.

Knit together one stitch from front needle and one stitch from back needle.

Bind off.

Substituting Yarns

All of the patterns in this book use basic yarn weights—bulky, heavy worsted, worsted, light worsted, and DK. Most of the yarns used in the book are available in many yarn stores or on the Internet. But if you want to substitute another yarn, here are some tips for making the transition as easy as possible.

When you look at the pattern, the first thing you will check is the yarn listed in the materials list. The name of the yarn, the manufacturer, the yardage, and the weight as well as the fiber content will be listed. Below that are the recommended needle sizes and the other materials needed for the garment and then the very important stitch gauge.

The three things you are most concerned about when substituting yarns are the yardage and weight of a skein, the recommended needle sizes, and the stitch and row gauge. In general, the yarn yardage is more important than the weight. The reason for this is that the fiber content of the yarn can affect the yardage. For example, alpaca is heavier than wool, so a 50 gram skein of wool is going to have more yardage than a 50 gram skein of alpaca. So if you are substituting alpaca for wool, you may need more skeins of yarn than what is listed.

Here is an example of how to calculate the yardage and the number of skeins so that you can purchase the correct number of skeins.

• The pattern calls for 10 skeins of a yarn that has 120 yards per 50 gram skein. Total yards: 10 skeins times 120 yards = 1200 yards.

• The yarn you want to use has 110 yards per 50 gram skein.

• Divide the number of yards per skein of the new yarn into the total yardage used in the pattern. In this case 1200 yards divided by 110 yards equal 10.90 skeins. You can't buy .9 of a skein so you would need 11 skeins.

One thing to remember is that when the number of skeins required is given in a pattern, you don't know how much of the last skein was actually used. It might be all of it or a little bit of it. I am a firm believer in the idea that it doesn't hurt to buy a little extra. This allows you to knit a large gauge swatch and keep it, as well as giving you some reassurance that you won't run out. And if you buy yarn and don't get to knit it right away, you don't have to worry about running out and not being able to match the dye lot or find the yarn, if it has been discontinued.

One of the major reasons that you might run out of yarn is that if your stitch and row gauge varies slightly from what is given in the pattern, you will use more yarn. This happens frequently with row gauge. It's pretty difficult to count in the first place, and it will vary from knitter to knitter. Since we do a lot of measuring instead of counting rows, it all seems to work just fine, but when the calculations were done to create the different sizes in a pattern, they were based on the stitch and row gauge given.

The next thing to look at when you are looking for a different yarn than that listed is the recommended needle size. Also check the gauge the yarn is supposed to knit at according to the label. They should be the same as or very close to what is listed in the pattern.

And finally, you will need to knit a gauge swatch to make sure the yarn you want to use works up to the gauge listed in the pattern. No fudging—$4\frac{3}{4}$ stitches to the inch is not the same as 5 stitches to the inch. Let's look at the math. Say you are supposed to have 100 stitches at 5 stitches to the inch. The width of the knitting would measure 20". 100 divided by 5 equals 20. But if you were really getting 4¾ stitches to the inch, the piece would measure 21"; that's 1" bigger than intended in the pattern. Accounting for 1" on the front and 1" on the back means your garment would be 2" larger than it is supposed to be. So to avoid the heartache, make your gauge swatch at least 8" x 8". I know that's a lot, but it will give you time to learn the pattern, get the feel for the yarn, and give you a very accurate measurement for your gauge.

With all of that done and the correct stitch gauge obtained, you can confidently substitute yarns and know you will be pleased with the finished vest.

Below is a list of the general weights of yarn and their recommended stitch gauge and yardage. This will also help you to choose yarns for substitution.

Choosing the Correct Size

The finished measurements given for each of the vests in this book are the actual size of the garment, not the bust measurement. The ease for the garment is included in this measurement. Do not use your bust measurement to choose your size. One of the best ways to choose the correct size in any knitting pattern is to measure something you own that is similar in size and weight to the garment you have chosen to knit. Then choose the size that most closely approximates the measurement of your own garment.

Pattern Tips and Tricks

Below are some tips to help you understand the directions when knitting the patterns. These tips should clear up any confusion you may experience when

reading these patterns or any other knitting pattern.

• Work decreases one stitch from the beginning or end of the row, unless the pattern states otherwise. The one stitch will act as a seam allowance for weaving seams or picking up stitches.

• Work slip, slip, knit (SSK) at the beginning of the row and knit two together (K2tog) at the end of the row for mirror-image decreases.

• Increases should also be worked leaving one stitch as a seam allowance. For example, when you are directed to use a make 1 (M1) increase, it has to be worked between two stitches, which means it cannot be worked on the first stitch or last stitch of a row. This increase will automatically leave a one-stitch seam allowance.

• When you are directed to end with a certain row—for example, the direction says "end with a

General Weights of Yarn, Gauge, Needle Size, and Yardage

Yarn	Gauge /4"	Needle size (approximate)	Yardage/100 g
Bulky	12 to 15 sts	10 to 11	110 to 120
Heavy Worsted	16 to 18 sts	9 to 10	120 to 140
Worsted	18 to 20 sts	7 to 8	200 to 220
Light Worsted	20 to 22 sts	7 to 8	220 to 240
DK	22 to 24 sts	5 to 6	250 to 275

Note: The weights of yarn are listed with each pattern. A different stitch guage may have been used to create the garment. This is for general reference only.

wrong-side row"—this means complete the wrong-side row and be ready to work a right-side row for the next direction.

• Work buttonholes on right front edge for women and on left front edge for men.

• Always bind off in pattern. If you have a K2, P2 ribbing, then you have to continue to work the K2, P2 as you bind off.

• To bind off loosely, use a needle two sizes larger than you have been using in the right hand as you work the bind off. Do not tug down on the yarn as you bind off.

• Don't assume or read into the pattern. If you've knit a similar pattern, it doesn't mean that everything will be the same. Read each line and make notes if necessary to make it as easy as possible.

• If there is a pattern stitch, mark down the rows or keep track in some way. It will save you a lot of grief later.

• And finally, learn to read your knitting. Mark the right side of the piece with a safety pin or piece of yarn if you are having trouble distinguishing the right side of the piece. When you have completed part of the pattern, look at it and learn to recognize the stitches and the patterns. Don't just knit blindly without looking at your work. Be sure you end the row with the correct number of stitches as given in the stitch pattern. After you decrease for the armhole, keep a close eye to be sure you are maintaining the pattern stitch.

Knitting Abbreviations

beg	begin(ning)
BO	bind off
CC	contrasting color
cn	cable needle
CO	cast on
cont	continue
dec	decrease
EOR	every other row
g	grams
inc	increase
K	knit
K2tog	knit 2 together
M1	make 1 stitch
MC	main color
P	purl
PM	place marker
PSSO	pass slipped stitch over
P2SSO	pass 2 slipped stitches over
PU	pick up and knit
rem	remaining
rep	repeat
RS	right side
sl st	slip stitch
SSK	slip, slip, knit
SSP	slip, slip, purl
st(s)	stitch(es)
St st	stockinette stitch
tog	together
W and T	wrap and turn
wyib	with yarn in back
wyif	with yarn in front
WS	wrong side
yds	yards
YO	yarn over

Multi-Size Vest for Men and Women

PLEASE DON'T let this pattern scare you. When you look at it, it looks crazy with all of the numbers lined up on the right and the directions on the left. It is a fill-in-the-blank pattern, and once you get used to it, you'll see that it is a very efficient way to write a pattern for multiple sizes and weights of yarn. It is simple to follow once you understand how it works. The best part about it is that each pattern gives you the option of making a pullover or cardigan vest in five sizes and four weights of yarn. With that many combinations available on each pattern, the possibilities are endless for making the correct size in any weight yarn or in any style you choose.

Using This Pattern

Follow these steps to help you work with these patterns.

1. Make a photocopy of the relevant chart on pages 16–29.

2. Choose the weight of yarn you want to use. Once you have obtained the stitch gauge, then all of the numbers in the column below that stitch gauge and weight of yarn are all you are concerned with. The numbers in the other columns refer to three other weights of yarn. One of the problems with having the extra columns is that your eye might jump to the wrong number. So either highlight the column you are using or block out the three columns you aren't using. Next mark the size you are making. You will refer to only the numbers for your size within the column. If a number is given only once, it refers to all of the sizes in the column.

Multi-Size Vest for Women (

Skill Level: Beginner
Sizes: S (M, L, XL, XXL)
Finished Chest: 34 (38, 42, 46, 50)"
Finished Length: 20½ (22, 23, 24½, 26)"

GAUGE: worked on larger needle in St st	4½ sts, 6 rows = 1"	4 sts, 6 rows = 1"	3½ sts, 4 rows =1"
SUPPLIES			
Yarn *Pastaza*	Naturally Tussock Aran 10 ply	Cascade Yarn Pastaza	Brown Sheep Bulky
Yards and grams per skein 5	172 yds, 100 g	132 yds, 100 g	125 yds, 113 g
Fiber content	85% NZ wool, 15% polyester	50% llama, 50% wool	85% wool/15% mohair
Number skeins required for cardigan or pullover	4 (5, 5, 6, 7)	4 (5, 5, 6, 7)	4 (4, 5, 5, 6)
Color number *044 Deep Blue*	169	1010	M-145
Needle sizes *7 + 9*	6 and 8	7 and 9	9 and 10½
29" circular needle size for cardigan *7*	6	7	9
Stitch holders *4*	4	4	4
½" to ¾" buttons for cardigan *5*	5 (5, 5, 6, 6)	5 (5, 5, 6, 6)	5 (5, 5, 6, 6)
Knitter's safety pin for V-neck cardigan	1	1	1
BACK FOR ALL STYLES			
*With smaller needle, CO *75* sts.	66 (76, 84, 94, 102)	59 (67, 75, 83, 91)	54 (62, 68, 76, 82)
Work border for *2½*".	2½ (2½, 3, 3, 3½)	2 (2¼, 2½, 3, 3¼)	1 (1, 1½, 1½, 2)
Sample border knit in *K1P1 rib*	K2, P2 ribbing	K1, P1 ribbing	Garter stitch
Inc *9* sts on last WS row of border.	10	9	5
Total sts *84*	76 (86, 94, 104, 112)	68 (76, 84, 92, 100)	59 (67, 73, 81, 87)
Change to larger needle and work St st until work measures *14*" to underarm*, beg armhole shaping.	12 (13, 14, 15, 16)	12 (13, 14, 15, 16)	12 (13, 14, 15, 16)
ARMHOLE SHAPING			
BO *11* sts at beg of next 2 rows.	8 (9, 10, 11, 12)	10 (10, 11, 12, 12)	7 (8, 8, 9, 10)
Dec 1 st at each end EOR *4* times.	5 (6, 7, 8, 9)	3 (4, 4, 5, 6)	4 (4, 5, 6, 6)
When armhole measures *8*", beg neck and shoulder shaping.	7½ (8, 8, 8½, 9)	7½ (8, 8, 8½, 9)	7½ (8, 8, 8½, 9)
BACK NECK AND RIGHT SHOULDER			
Work across *13* sts of right shoulder. Leave rem sts on left	12 (14, 15, 16, 17)	9 (11, 13, 14, 15)	9 (11, 13, 14)
Dec 1 st at neck edge on RS *1* time(s).	2	1	1
When armhole measures *9*", beg short rows.	8½ (9, 9, 9½, 10)	8½ (9, 9, 9½, 10)	8½ (9, 9, 9½, 10)
Work purl-side short-row *6* sts from armhole edge (pg 8)	5 (5, 6, 6, 7)	4 (5, 6, 6, 7)	4 (5, 6, 6, 7)
Work one row to retrieve wraps from short rows. Place all sts			

Continued on page 18

3. The directions on the left have blank spaces for you to fill in with the correct number from the columns at the right. Using the numbers in the column you have chosen and the size you have chosen, write the numbers in with pencil (in case you make a mistake or want to use the pattern again). This will keep your eye from wandering to the wrong column and possibly picking the wrong numbers and making a mistake.

4. I have used a different border for each pattern; they are all interchangeable. You may need to make a slight adjustment in the number of stitches to cast on for the border so that the border works out correctly. For example, in K2, P2 ribbing you need to have a multiple of four stitches, plus two edge stitches for the seams. Any adjustment you make in the number of stitches to the cast on can then be adjusted when the increases are made above the border, before proceeding with stockinette stitch for the rest of the vest.

5. The charts are given for men and women. But, let's say you're a woman and the finished chest size you need is on the men's chart. You can use that set of instructions, adjusting the length and armhole depth if necessary.

6. You can adjust any of the lengths for any of the sizes. Just be sure you account for the change when picking up stitches for the front bands of the cardigans. In other words, if you make the side seam shorter, you would pick up fewer stitches to the V neck for a cardigan, or if you make it longer you would pick up more stitches. The button-hole placement would have to adjust slightly as well.

7. Working the short-row shaping for the shoulders is very important. Don't leave this step out. See pages 7 and 8 for how to work the short rows.

8. Should you choose to substitute yarn for these vests, you should substitute another light worsted weight yarn for Dale of Norway Sisik; a worsted weight for Naturally Tussock Aran; a heavy worsted weight for Cascade Yarns Pastaza; and a bulky weight yarn for Brown Sheep Bulky.

Multi-Size Vest for Women (Pullover and Cardigan)

Skill Level: Beginner

Sizes: S (M, L, XL, XXL)

Finished Chest: 34 (38, 42, 46, 50)"

Finished Length: 20½ (22, 23, 24½, 26)"

GAUGE: worked on larger needle in St st	5 sts, 7 rows = 1"
SUPPLIES	
Yarn	Dale of Norway Sisik
Yards and grams per skein	148 yds, 50 g
Fiber content	30% wool, 30% mohair, 34% acrylic, 6% rayon
Number skeins required for cardigan or pullover	4 (4, 5, 6, 7)
Color number	1023
Needle sizes	5 and 7
29" circular needle size for cardigan	5
Stitch holders	4
½" to ¾" buttons for cardigan	5 (5, 5, 6, 6)
Knitter's safety pin for V-neck cardigan	1
BACK FOR ALL STYLES	
*With smaller needle, CO ____ sts.	75 (85, 95, 105, 115)
Work border for ____".	1 (1¼, 1½, 1½, 2)
Sample border knit in ____.	Seed stitch
Inc ____ sts on last WS row of border.	10
Total sts	85 (95, 105, 115, 125)
Change to larger needle and work St st until work measures ____" to underarm*, beg armhole shaping.	12 (13, 14, 15, 16)
ARMHOLE SHAPING	
BO ____ sts at beg of next 2 rows.	12 (12, 14, 16, 18)
Dec 1 st at each end EOR ____ times.	4 (4, 5, 6, 7)
When armhole measures____", beg neck and shoulder shaping.	7½ (8, 8, 8½, 9)
BACK NECK AND RIGHT SHOULDER	
Work across ____ sts of right shoulder. Leave rem sts on left needle.	12 (15, 16, 17, 18)
Dec 1 st at neck edge on RS ____ time(s).	2
When armhole measures ____", beg short rows.	8½ (9, 9, 9½, 10)
Work purl-side short-row ____ sts from armhole edge (pg 8).	5 (6, 7, 7, 8)
Work one row to retrieve wraps from short rows. Place all sts on holder.	

4½ sts, 6 rows = 1"	4 sts, 6 rows = 1"	3½ sts, 4 rows =1"
Naturally Tussock Aran 10 ply	Cascade Yarn Pastaza	Brown Sheep Bulky
172 yds, 100 g	132 yds, 100 g	125 yds, 113 g
85% NZ wool, 15% polyester	50% llama, 50% wool	85% wool/15% mohair
4 (5, 5, 6, 7)	4 (5, 5, 6, 7)	4 (4, 5, 5, 6)
169	1010	M-145
6 and 8	7 and 9	9 and 10½
6	7	9
4	4	4
5 (5, 5, 6, 6)	5 (5, 5, 6, 6)	5 (5, 5, 6, 6)
1	1	1
66 (76, 84, 94, 102)	59 (67, 75, 83, 91)	54 (62, 68, 76, 82)
2½ (2½, 3, 3, 3½)	2 (2¼, 2½, 3, 3¼)	1 (1, 1½, 1½, 2)
K2, P2 ribbing	K1, P1 ribbing	Garter stitch
10	9	5
76 (86, 94, 104, 112)	68 (76, 84, 92, 100)	59 (67, 73, 81, 87)
12 (13, 14, 15, 16)	12 (13, 14, 15, 16)	12 (13, 14, 15, 16)
8 (9, 10, 11, 12)	10 (10, 11, 12, 12)	7 (8, 8, 9, 10)
5 (6, 7, 8, 9)	3 (4, 4, 5, 6)	4 (4, 5, 6, 6)
7½ (8, 8, 8½, 9)	7½ (8, 8, 8½, 9)	7½ (8, 8, 8½, 9)
12 (14, 15, 16, 17)	9 (11, 13, 14, 15)	9 (11, 13, 14, 14)
2	1	1
8½ (9, 9, 9½, 10)	8½ (9, 9, 9½, 10)	8½ (9, 9, 9½, 10)
5 (5, 6, 6, 7)	4 (5, 6, 6, 7)	4 (5, 6, 6, 7)

Continued on page 18

Multi-Size Vest for Women (Pullover and Cardigan) *continued*

GAUGE: worked on larger needle in St st	5 sts, 7 rows = 1"
BACK NECK AND LEFT SHOULDER	
Rejoin yarn with RS facing.	
BO ____ sts for back neck, finish row.	29 (33, 35, 37, 39)
Dec 1 st at neck edge on RS ____ time(s).	2
Beg short-row shaping for shoulders.	
Work knit-side short-row ____ sts from armhole edge (pg 7).	5 (6, 7, 7, 8)
Work one row to retrieve wraps from short rows. Place all sts on holder.	
V-NECK PULLOVER FRONTS	
Work from * to * of back for all sizes.	
Beg armhole shaping as for back and **at same time** work V-neck shaping.	
Place ctr ____ sts on knitter's safety pin. Working each side separately,	1
Dec 1 st at neck edge EOR ____ times,	8 (9, 10, 11, 12)
then every 4th row ____ times.	8 (9, 9, 9, 9)
When armhole measures same as back, work short rows as for back.	
FINISHING	
Work 3-needle BO to seam shoulders.	
Weave side seams together.	
NECKBAND	
With smaller circular needle, beg at right shoulder seam,	
PU ____ sts to left shoulder seam,	37 (41, 43, 45, 47)
PU ____ sts to center front,	50 (54, 54, 57, 60)
Knit ____ sts from safety pin,	1
PU ____ from safety pin,	after stitch
PU ___ sts to right shoulder seam, PM.	50 (54, 54, 57, 60)
Work chosen border for ____ row.	1
Work remaining ____ rows as follows:	6 (6, 6, 7, 7)
Work to ____ sts before marker, K2 tog,	3
Slip marker, K ____ sts, SSK, finish row.	1
Keep continuity of border pattern after dec.	
BO all sts loosely, finish off.	
ARMHOLE BANDS	
With smaller size circular needle, beg at underarm seam,	
PU ____ sts to shoulder, and rep for other side.	37 (41, 43, 45, 47)
Work chosen border for ____ rows. BO all sts.	8 (8, 8, 10, 10)

4½ sts, 6 rows = 1"	4 sts, 6 rows = 1"	3½ sts, 4 rows =1"
26 (28, 30, 34, 36)	24 (26, 28, 30, 34)	21 (23, 25, 27, 29)
2	1	1
5 (5, 6, 6, 7)	4 (5, 6, 6, 7)	4 (5, 6, 6, 7)
2	2	3
10 (10, 11, 13, 14)	6 (7, 8, 8, 9)	5 (6, 6, 7, 7)
4 (5, 5, 5, 5)	6 (6, 6, 7, 8)	5 (5, 6, 6, 7)
30 (34, 36, 38, 42)	26 (28, 30, 32, 36)	28 (30, 32, 34, 36)
42 (50, 52, 54, 54)	44 (48, 50, 54, 56)	30 (34, 34, 36, 38)
2	2	3
between the 2 sts	between the 2 sts	after first st
42 (50, 52, 54, 54)	44 (48, 50, 54, 56)	30 (34, 34, 36, 38)
1	1	1
5 (5, 5, 7, 7)	3 (3, 5, 5, 7)	3 (3, 5, 5, 7)
2	2	2
0	0	1
42 (50, 50, 52, 56)	30 (34, 34, 36, 38)	38 (40, 40, 42, 44)
6 (6, 6, 8, 8)	6 (6, 6, 8, 8)	4 (4, 6, 6, 8)

Continued on page 20

Multi-Size Vest for Women (Pullover and Cardigan) *continued*

GAUGE: worked on larger needle in St st	**5 sts, 7 rows = 1"**
V-NECK CARDIGAN LEFT FRONT	
*With smaller needle, CO ____ sts.	38 (42, 48, 54, 58)
Work border for ____ ".	1 (1¼, 1½, 1½, 2)
Inc ____ sts on last WS row of border.	4
Total sts	42 (46, 52, 58, 62)
Change to larger needle and work St st until work measures ____ " to underarm*, beg armhole and V neck shaping.	12 (13, 14, 15, 16)
ARMHOLE AND V-NECK SHAPING	
BO ____ sts at beg of next 2 rows.	12 (12, 14, 16, 18)
Dec 1 st at each end EOR ____ times.	4 (4, 5, 6, 7)
At same time, beg neck shaping.	
Dec 1 st at neck edge EOR ____ times,	10 (11, 13, 14, 14)
then every 4th row ____ times.	6 (6, 6, 7, 7)
When armhole measures ____ ", beg shoulder shaping.	7½ (8, 8, 8½, 9)
SHOULDER SHAPING	
Beg short-row shaping for shoulders.	
Work purl-side short-row ____ sts from armhole edge (pg 8).	5 (6, 7, 7, 8)
Work 1 row to retrieve wraps from short row. Place sts on holder.	
V-NECK CARDIGAN RIGHT FRONT	
Work as for left front, reversing shaping.	
FINISHING	
Work 3-needle BO to seam shoulders.	
Weave side seams together.	
Work armhole borders as for back.	
FRONT BAND AND V-NECK BORDERS	
Beg at right front lower edge with smaller circ needle,	
PU ____ sts to start of V neck,	66 (68, 68, 70, 74)
PU ____ sts to right shoulder seam,	50 (54, 54, 57, 60)
Knit ____ sts across back neck,	37 (41, 43, 45, 47)
PU ____ sts to beg of V neck of left front,	50 (54, 54, 57, 60)
PU ____ sts to lower edge.	66 (68, 68, 70, 74)
Work border for ____ rows.	3 (3, 5, 5, 5)
BUTTONHOLES	
On right front (RS facing) work buttonholes:	
Work ____ sts, *K2tog, YO,	4 (4, 6, 6, 6)
Work ____ sts*,	12 (13, 12, 10, 11)
rep from * to * ____ more times.	4 (4, 4, 5, 5)
Work ____ more rows.	3
BO loosely.	

For all vests: Weave in all ends. Steam gently if the yarn is a wool or wool blend. Moisten and allow to dry if the yarn is cotton or a synthetic fiber. For cardigans: Sew on buttons with matching sewing thread.

4½ sts, 6 rows = 1"	4 sts, 6 rows = 1"	3½ sts, 4 rows =1"
34 (38, 42, 48, 52)	29 (33, 37, 41, 45)	28 (32, 36, 38, 42)
2½ (2½, 3, 3, 3½)	2 (2¼, 2½, 3, 3¼)	1 (1, 1½, 1½, 2)
5	5	2
39 (43, 47, 53, 57)	34 (38, 42, 46, 50)	30 (34, 38, 40, 44)
12 (13, 14, 15, 16)	12 (13, 14, 15, 16)	12 (13, 14, 15, 16)
8 (9, 10, 11, 12)	10 (10, 11, 12, 12)	7 (8, 8, 9, 10)
5 (6, 7, 8, 9)	3 (4, 4, 5, 6)	4 (4, 5, 6, 6)
12 (12, 13, 16, 17)	7 (8, 9, 9, 11)	12 (13, 15, 14, 16)
4 (4, 4, 4, 4)	6 (6, 6, 7, 7)	0 (0, 0, 0, 0)
7½ (8, 8, 8½, 9)	7½ (8, 8, 8½, 9)	7½ (8, 8, 8½, 9)
5 (5, 6, 6, 7)	4 (5, 6, 6, 7)	4 (5, 6, 6, 7)
56 (58, 60, 62, 64)	56 (58, 60, 62, 64)	36 (40, 40, 42, 44)
44 (48, 50, 54, 56)	44 (48, 50, 54, 56)	30 (34, 34, 36, 38)
30 (32, 34, 38, 40)	30 (32, 34, 38, 40)	28 (30, 32, 34, 36)
44 (48, 50, 54, 56)	44 (48, 50, 54, 56)	30 (34, 34, 36, 38)
56 (58, 60, 62, 64)	56 (58, 60, 62, 64)	36 (40, 40, 42, 44)
3 (3, 5, 5, 5)	3 (3, 3, 3, 3)	3 (3, 3, 3, 3)
4 (4, 6, 6, 6)	4 (4, 6, 6, 6)	4 (4, 4, 4, 4)
10 (11, 11, 8, 9)	10 (11, 11, 8, 9)	5 (5, 6, 5, 5)
4 (4, 4, 5, 5)	4 (4, 4, 5, 5)	4 (4, 4, 5, 5)
2	2	1

Continued on page 22

Multi-Size Vest for Men (Pullover and Cardigan)

Skill Level: Beginner

Sizes: S (M, L, XL, XXL)

Finished Chest: 40 (44, 46, 50, 54)"

Finished Length: 23 (24½, 26, 26½, 28)"

Gauge: worked on larger needle in St st	**5 sts, 7 rows = 1"**
SUPPLIES	
Yarn	Dale of Norway Sisik
Yards and grams per skein	148 yds, 50 g
Fiber content	30% wool, 30% mohair, 34% acrylic, 6% rayon
Number skeins required for cardigan or pullover	5 (6, 7, 7, 8)
Color number	1023
Needle sizes	5 and 7
29" circular needle size ____ for cardigans	5
Stitch holders	4
¾" buttons for cardigan	5 (5, 5, 6, 6)
BACK FOR ALL STYLES	
*With smaller needle, CO ____ sts.	90 (100, 110, 120, 130)
Work border for ____".	1 (1¼, 1½, 1½, 2)
Sample border knit in ____ .	Seed stitch
Inc ____ sts on last WS row of border.	10
Total sts	100 (110, 120, 130, 140)
Change to larger needle and work in St st until work ____ " to underarm*, beg armhole shaping.	14 (15, 16, 16, 17)
ARMHOLE SHAPING	
BO ____ sts at beg of next 2 rows.	5 (6, 7, 10, 10)
BO ____ sts at beg of next 2 rows.	4 (5, 6, 8, 8)
Dec 1 st at each end EOR ____ times.	4 (4, 5, 4, 5)
When armhole measures ____ ", beg neck and shoulder shaping.	8 (8½ 9, 9½, 10)
BACK NECK AND RIGHT SHOULDER	
Work across ____ sts of right shoulder. Leave rem sts on left needle.	20 (23, 24, 24, 27)
Dec 1 st at neck edge on RS ____ time(s).	2
When armhole measures ____", beg purl-side short rows (pg 8).	9 (9½, 10, 10½, 11)
Work 1st short row ____ sts from armhole edge.	7 (8, 8, 8, 9)
Work 2nd short row ____ sts from prev short row.	6 (6, 8, 8, 9)
Work one row to retrieve wraps from short rows. Place all sts on holder.	

4½ sts, 6 rows = 1"	4 sts, 6 rows = 1"	3½ sts, 4 rows = 1"
Naturally Tussock Aran	Cascade Yarn Pastaza	Brown Sheep Bulky
172 yds, 100 g	132 yds, 100 g	125 yds, 113 g
85% NZ wool, 15% polyester	50% llama, 50% wool	85% wool, 15% mohair
5 (6, 6, 7, 8)	5 (5, 6, 7, 8)	5 (5, 6, 7, 8)
169	1010	M-145
6 and 8	7 and 9	9 and 10½
6	7	9
4	4	4
5 (5, 5, 6, 6)	5 (5, 5, 6, 6)	5 (5, 5, 6, 6)
80 (90, 98, 108, 116)	72 (80, 88, 96, 104))	63 (71, 77, 85, 91)
2½ (2½, 3, 3, 3½)	2 (2¼, 2½, 3, 3¼)	1 (1, 1½, 1½, 2)
K2, P2 ribbing	K1, P1 ribbing	Garter stitch
10	8	8
90 (100, 108, 118, 126)	80 (88, 96, 104, 112)	71 (79, 85, 93, 99)
14 (15, 16, 16, 17)	14 (15, 16, 16, 17)	14 (15, 16, 16, 17)
7 (9, 10, 11, 12)	5 (6, 7, 8, 9)	5 (5, 5, 5, 5)
2 (4, 4, 5, 5)	3 (4, 4, 5, 5)	2 (3, 3, 4, 4)
2 (3, 3, 3, 4)	3 (3, 3, 4, 4)	3 (4, 4, 6, 6)
8 (8½ 9, 9½, 10)	8 (8½ 9, 9½, 10)	8 (8½ 9, 9½, 10)
18 (20, 22, 24, 24)	15 (17, 19, 19, 21)	13 (15, 17, 17, 19)
2	1	1
9 (9½, 10, 10½, 11)	9 (9½, 10, 10½, 11)	9 (9½, 10, 10½, 11)
5 (6, 7, 8, 8)	5 (6, 7, 7, 8)	6 (7, 8, 8, 9)
5 (6, 7, 8, 8)	5 (6, 7, 7, 8)	0

Continued on page 24

Multi-Size Vest for Men (Pullover and Cardigan) *continued*

Gauge: worked on larger needle in St st	**5 sts, 7 rows = 1"**
ARMHOLE BANDS	
With smaller size circular needle, beg at underarm seam,	
PU _____ sts to shoulder seam and rep for other side.	52 (55, 59, 63, 66)
Work chosen border for _____ rows. BO.	6 (6, 6, 8, 8)
V-NECK CARDIGAN LEFT FRONT	
With smaller needle, CO _____ sts.	44 (50, 54, 60, 64)
Work border for _____",	1 (1¼, 1½, 1½, 2)
Inc _____ sts on last WS row of border.	6
Total sts	50 (56, 60, 66, 70)
Change to larger needle and work in St st until work measures _____" to underarm.	14 (15, 16, 16, 17)
ARMHOLE AND V-NECK SHAPING	
BO _____ sts at armhole edge,	5 (6, 7, 10, 10)
BO _____ sts at armhole edge,	4 (5, 6, 8, 8)
Dec 1 st at at armhole edge EOR _____ times.	4 (4, 5, 4, 5)
At same time beg neck shaping:	
Dec 1 st at neck edge EOR _____ times,	12 (13, 11, 12, 11)
then every 4th row _____ times.	7 (7, 9, 10, 11)
When armhole measures _____", beg shoulder shaping.	8 (8½ 9, 9½, 10)
SHOULDER SHAPING	
Work purl-side short-row shaping for shoulders (pg 8).	
Work 1st short row _____ sts from armhole edge.	7 (8, 8, 8, 9)
Work 2nd short row _____ sts from prev short row.	6 (6, 8, 8, 9)
Work one row to retrieve wraps from short rows. Place all sts on holder.	
V-NECK CARDIGAN RIGHT FRONT	
Work as for left front, reversing shaping.	
FINISHING	
Work 3-needle BO to seam shoulders.	
Weave side seams together.	
Work armhole borders as given for back.	

4½ sts, 6 rows = 1"	4 sts, 6 rows = 1"	3½ sts, 4 rows = 1"
48 (50, 53, 54, 58)	48 (50, 53, 54, 58)	36 (38, 40, 42, 44)
5 (5, 6, 7, 7)	5 (5, 6, 6, 6)	4 (4, 6, 6, 6)
42 (46, 50, 54, 60)	35 (39, 43, 47, 51)	31 (35, 39, 41, 45)
2½ (2½, 3, 3, 3½)	2 (2¼, 2½, 3, 3¼)	1 (1, 1½, 1½, 2)
4	5	4
46 (50, 54, 58, 64)	40 (44, 48, 52, 56)	35 (39, 43, 45, 49)
14 (15, 16, 16, 17)	14 (15, 16, 16, 17)	14 (15, 16, 16, 17)
7 (9, 10, 11, 12)	5 (6, 7, 8, 9)	5 (5, 5, 5, 5)
2 (4, 4, 5, 5)	3 (4, 4, 5, 5)	2 (3, 3, 4, 4)
2 (3, 3, 3, 4)	3 (3, 3, 4, 4)	3 (4, 4, 6, 6)
17 (16, 17, 17, 21)	15 (15, 16, 17, 18)	11 (10, 12, 11, 12)
0	0	2 (3, 3, 3, 4)
8 (8½, 9, 9½, 10)	8 (8½, 9, 9½, 10)	8 (8½, 9, 9½, 10)
5 (6, 7, 8, 8)	5 (6, 7, 7, 8)	6 (7, 8, 8, 9)
5 (6, 7, 8, 8)	5 (6, 7, 7, 8)	0

Continued on page 28

Gauge: worked on larger needle in St st | **5 sts, 7 rows = 1"**

FRONT BAND AND V-NECK BORDERS

Starting at right front lower edge with smaller circular needle,	
PU ____ sts to start of V neck,	75 (80, 83, 83, 88)
PU ____ sts to right shoulder seam,	52 (55, 59, 63, 66)
Knit ____ sts across back neck,	40 (40, 42, 44, 46)
PU ____ sts to beg of V neck on left front,	52 (55, 59, 63, 66)
PU ____ sts to lower edge.	75 (80, 83, 83, 88)
Work border for ____ rows.	4 (4, 4, 6, 6)

BUTTONHOLES

On left front (WS facing), work buttonholes as follows:	
Work ____ sts, *K2tog, YO,	4 (4, 6, 6, 6)
Work ____ sts*,	15 (16, 17, 13, 14)
rep from * to * ____ more times.	4 (4, 4, 5, 5)
Work ____ more rows.	2 (2, 4, 4, 4)
BO loosely.	

For all vests: Weave in all ends. Steam gently if the yarn is a wool or wool blend. Moisten and allow to dry if the yarn is cotton or a synthetic fiber.
For cardigans: Sew on buttons with matching sewing thread.

4½ sts, 6 rows = 1"	4 sts, 6 rows = 1"	3½ sts, 4 rows = 1"
64 (66, 70, 70, 76)	64 (66, 70, 70, 76)	56 (58, 60, 60, 64)
44 (46, 48, 50, 52)	44 (46, 48, 50, 52)	36 (38, 40, 42, 44)
34 (34, 36, 38, 44)	32 (32, 34, 36, 38)	29 (29, 31, 33, 35)
44 (46, 48, 50, 52)	44 (46, 48, 50, 52)	36 (38, 40, 42, 44)
64 (66, 70, 70, 76)	64 (66, 70, 70, 76)	56 (58, 60, 60, 64)
4 (4, 4, 6, 6)	2 (2, 2, 4, 4)	2 (2, 2, 4, 4)
4 (4, 6, 6, 6)	4 (4, 6, 6, 6)	4 (4, 6, 6, 6)
12 (13, 14, 13, 15)	12 (13, 14, 13, 15)	10 (11, 11, 8, 9)
4 (4, 4, 5, 5)	4 (4, 4, 5, 5)	4 (4, 4, 5, 5)
2 (2, 3, 3, 3)	2 (2, 3, 3, 3)	1 (1, 3, 3, 3)

Friday Harbor

Simple garter stitch and a "new" button loop create this simple but wonderful-to-wear design for men and women. Very little finishing will help you breeze through this vest. You'll be done in no time.

Skill Level: Beginner

Sizes: Small (Medium, Large, X-Large, XX-Large)

Finished Chest: 34½ (38, 42½, 46, 52½)"

Finished Length: 21 (22, 23½, 25, 26½)"

Materials

7 (8, 9, 11, 13) skeins Gypsy from Reynolds (100% mercerized cotton; 82 yds, 50 g per skein), color 420, or other light worsted weight yarn

Size 5 needles (or size required to obtain gauge)

4 stitch holders

5 buttons, ¾" diameter

Gauge

18 sts and 32 rows = 4" in garter stitch on size 5 needles

Notes: Count the ridges of the garter st to help you make the fronts match the back in length.

Sl all sts as if to knit wyib at beg of every row.

Back

- CO 78 (86, 96, 104, 118) sts. Work garter st until piece measures 12 (13, 14, 15, 16)".

- **Armholes:** BO 8 (9, 10, 10, 10) sts at beg of next 2 rows, dec 1 st at each end EOR 6 (6, 7, 8, 9) times—50 (56, 62, 68, 80) sts. Cont until armhole measures 8½ (8½, 9, 9½, 10)", ending on WS row.

- **Neck:** Work across 11 (13, 15, 17, 21) sts, BO center 28 (30, 32, 34, 38) sts, cont across 11 (13, 15, 17, 21) sts.

- **Left shoulder:** Knit 1 row (WS). Beg short-row shaping on next RS row, K7 (8, 9, 11, 13) sts, W and T, knit back. K3 (4, 4, 6, 8) sts, W and T, knit back. Knit 1 row to retrieve wraps. Knit 1 more row. Place sts on stitch holder.

- **Right shoulder:** Reattach yarn at neck edge with WS facing. Knit 2 rows. Beg short-row shaping on next WS row, K7 (8, 9, 11, 13) sts, W and T, knit back. K3 (4, 5, 6, 7) sts, W and T, knit back. Knit 1 row to retrieve wraps. Place sts on stitch holder.

Left Front

- *CO 42 (46, 51, 55, 62) sts. Work as for back to armhole shaping, ending on WS row.

- **Armhole and V neck:** BO 8 (9, 10, 10, 10) sts at armhole edge, dec 1 st at armhole edge EOR 6 (6, 7, 8, 9) times. *At same time*, dec 1 st at neck edge every 4th row 14 (14, 15, 15, 16) times, then EOR 3 (4, 4, 5, 6) times—11 (13, 15, 17, 21) sts.

- **Shoulder:** Cont until armhole measures 8½ (8½, 9, 9½, 10)"*. Work short-row shaping as for back right shoulder.

Right Front

- Work from * to * of left front placing button loops as directed in sidebar on facing page. Work short-row shaping as for back left shoulder.

Finishing

- Work 3-needle BO for shoulders.

- Weave side seams tog.

- Mist heavily with water and allow to dry flat. Smooth gently while wet.

- Sew on buttons.

Button Loops

• Work button loops as follows while knitting right front. At the beg of RS row where buttonhole is to beg, using the cable cast on (see page 41), CO 6 sts, BO the same 6 sts (button loop created), cont across row. Knit 2 more rows, knit next row (WS) to last st, sl that st, pick up a st in the end of the tail of the button loop, be careful not to twist, PSSO. Cont knitting, counting the ridges from where the sts were CO for the button loop. Work first button loop 4 ridges from the bottom edge, and then every 10 (11, 12, 13, 13) ridges 4 times.

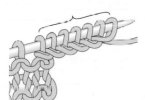

Cast on 6 sts.

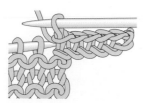

Bind off 6 sts.

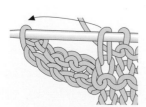

Pass slipped stitch over the picked-up stitch.

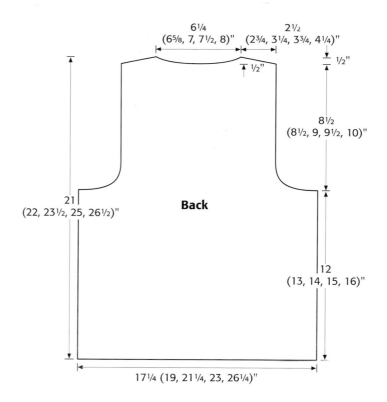

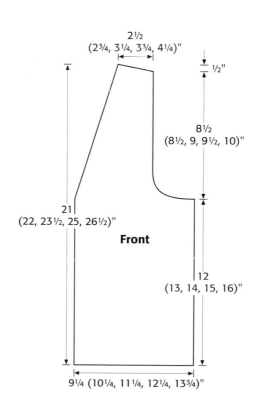

San Francisco

This rib-looking pattern is actually a slip-stitch pattern. There is no purling and no finishing, except for the four seams. Gee, what more could you ask for both men and women?

Skill Level: Advanced Beginner

Sizes: Small (Medium, Large, X-Large, XX-Large)

Finished Chest: 36 (41, 46, 51, 56)"

Finished Length: 20½ (22, 23½, 26, 27½)"

Materials

7 (7, 9, 11, 13) skeins Silk Garden from Noro (45% silk, 45% kid mohair, 10% lamb's wool; 110 yds, 50 g per skein), color 39, or other worsted weight yarn

Size 7 needles (or size required to obtain gauge)

4 stitch holders

Gauge

16 sts and 32 rows = 4" in pattern stitch on size 7 needles

Note: All of the skeins of the Noro yarn contain the same sequence of colors, but they may be wound in a different order. You will need to manipulate the yarn to make the stripes occur in the same order on the back and front. When you need to start another skein of yarn, you will have to start it using the next color in the sequence to keep the stripes in the same order. Meaning, you may have to roll a part of a skein into a ball to find the correct color to start the new skein. The yarn you rolled into a ball will then be used at the end of that skein. After the armhole is shaped, the colors will not stripe the same as before the armhole. But you will still need to start a skein in the same manner as above. Be sure to start each skein in the same direction. For example, pull all skeins from the inside.

Pattern Stitch

Multiple of 5 + 7.

Row 1: (WS) K3, sl 1 wyif, (K4, sl 1 wyif) to last 3 sts, end K3.

Row 2: Knit.

Rep rows 1 and 2.

Note: Sl all sts at beg of rows as if to knit. Sl all sts in patt as if to purl.

Back

• CO 72 (82, 92, 102, 112) sts. Work in patt until piece measures 12 (13, 14, 16, 17)".

• **Armholes:** BO 6 (7, 8, 9, 10) sts at each end, dec 1 st at each end EOR 4 (5, 6, 6, 7) times— 52 (58, 64, 72, 78) sts. Work until armhole measures 8 (8½, 9, 9½, 10)".

• **Neck:** Work across 15 (16, 17, 19, 21) sts, BO center 22 (26, 30, 34, 36) sts, work across rem 15 (16, 17, 19, 21) sts.

• **Left shoulder:** Work WS row. *Dec 1 st at neck edge on next RS row. Work WS row. Place rem 14 (15, 16, 18, 20) sts on stitch holder.

• **Right shoulder:** Rejoin yarn at neck edge with WS facing, work across. Work from * as for left shoulder.

Front

• Work as for back to armhole shaping. On next RS row, work across 36 (41, 46, 51, 56) sts, place rem 36 (41, 46, 51, 56) sts on stitch holder.

• **Left armhole and neck:** BO 6 (7, 8, 9, 10) sts at armhole edge, work to center, dec 1 st at neck edge every fourth row 10 (10, 9, 9, 9) times, then EOR 2 (4, 7, 9, 10) times and **at same time,** dec 1 st at armhole edge EOR 4 (5, 6, 6, 7) times—14 (15, 16, 18, 20) sts. Place rem sts on stitch holder.

• **Right armhole and neck:** Rejoin yarn at center front with RS facing, leaving a 14" tail. Work first neck edge dec as given for left armhole and neck. Work across, BO for armhole on next WS row. Cont with neck and armhole dec as for left armhole and neck.

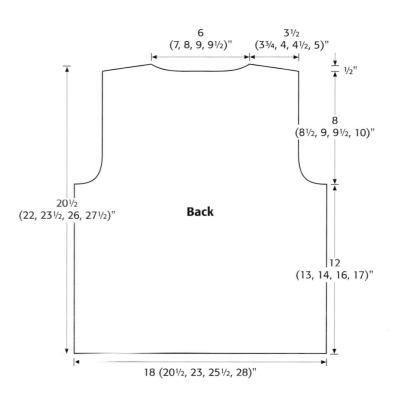

Finishing

• Work 3-needle BO for shoulders.

• Use 14" tail to reinforce V neck at center front by weaving yarn back and forth through center 5 sts below start of V neck. This will help keep the neck from stretching out of shape.

• Weave side seams tog.

• Lay flat, mist with water, smooth with your hand, and allow to dry completely before removing.

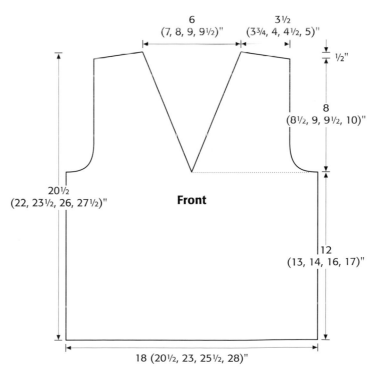

Chicago

A perfect vest for both men and women. There is very little finishing on this vest because the bands are knit in tandem with the body of the sweater. The large buttons are a great accent to the simply knit vest.

Skill Level: Advanced Beginner

Sizes: Small (Medium, Large, X-Large, XX-Large)

Finished Chest: 38 (42, 46, 50, 54)"

Finished Length: 21 (23, 24, 25½, 26½)"

Materials

4 (4, 5, 5, 6) skeins Magpie Tweed from Rowan (100% wool; 185 yds, 100 g per skein), color 778, or other heavy worsted weight yarn

Size 8 needles (or size required to obtain gauge)

2 stitch holders

5 (5, 5, 6, 6) buttons, 1" diameter

Ring markers

Gauge

14 sts and 28 rows = 4" in pattern stitch on size 8 needles

Pattern Stitch

Multiple of 2 + 1.

Row 1 (RS): Knit.

Row 2: (K1, P1) across to last st, K1.

Rep rows 1 and 2.

Back

• CO 67 (73, 81, 87, 95) sts, work in patt until piece measures 11 (12½, 13, 14, 15)".

• **Next 8 rows:** Work garter st over first and last 13 (13, 13, 15, 15) sts, keeping center sts in patt (PM to designate garter st sections).

• **Armhole:** BO 9 (9, 9, 11, 11) sts at beg of next 2 rows—49 (55, 63, 65, 73) sts. Keeping 4 sts in garter st at both edges throughout, cont until armhole measures 6¾ (7½, 7¾, 8, 8)".

• On next RS row, work across 8 (10, 13, 13, 16) sts, PM, work across next 33 (35, 37, 39, 41) sts, PM, work across rem 8 (10, 13, 13, 16) sts. Cont in pat, except work center sts designated by markers in garter st for 7 more rows.

• **Neck:** On next row, work to marker for center sts, K5, BO center 23 (25, 27, 29, 31) sts, K5, cont across rem 8 (10, 13, 13, 16) sts for ¾ (¾, 1, 1, 1)".

• **Left shoulder:** Cont where yarn is attached, work patt for 1 row, keeping 5 sts at neck edge in garter st. Cont until armhole measures 8½ (9, 9½, 10, 10)", ending on WS row. Beg short-row shaping on next RS row: K9

(10, 12, 12, 14) sts, W and T, work back in patt. K4 (5, 6, 6, 7) sts, W and T, work back in patt. Work one more row to retrieve wraps. BO all sts.

• **Right shoulder:** Reattach yarn at neck edge with WS facing. Keeping 5 sts at neck edge in garter st, work in patt until armhole measures 8½ (9, 9½, 10, 10)", ending on RS row. Beg short-row shaping on next WS row: Work 9 (10, 12, 12, 14) sts in patt, W and T, work back in patt. Work 4 (5, 6, 6, 7) sts in patt, W and T, work back in patt. Work one more row to retrieve wraps. BO all sts.

Pocket Linings
(make 2)

CO 17 (17, 21, 21, 23) sts, work in St st for 3 (3, 3½, 4, 4½)", work patt st for 1". Place sts on a holder.

Left Front

Buttonhole placement for men; see sidebar on facing page.

• CO 38 (42, 46, 48, 52) sts. K5, PM, work rem sts in patt st. Keeping 5 sts at center front in garter st, work until piece measures 6½ (7, 7, 8, 9)", ending on WS row.

• Work across 8 (10, 10, 11, 12) sts, PM, work across next 17 (17, 21, 21, 23) sts, PM, finish row. Work 5 (5, 5, 7, 7) rows, working sts inside markers in garter st. On next RS row, work to marker, BO sts between markers, cont across row. **Next row:** work across to bound off sts, with WS of pocket lining facing, place sts on left needle, work across pocket lining, keeping continuity of patt, finish row. Cont in patt until piece measures 11 (12½, 13, 14, 15)", ending on WS row.

- **Armhole:** Keeping 13 (13, 13, 15, 15) sts at armhole edge in garter st for 8 rows, work rem sts in patt. BO 9 (9, 9, 11, 11) sts at beg of next RS row—29 (33, 37, 37, 41) sts. Cont in patt until armhole measures 3½ (4, 4½, 4½, 4½)".

- **Neck:** On next WS row, K21 (23, 24, 24, 25) sts, PM, work rem of row in patt as established. Keeping 21 (23, 24, 24, 25) sts in garter st, work 7 more rows. BO 16 (18, 19, 19, 20) sts at neck edge—13 (15, 18, 18, 21) sts. Keeping 5 sts at neck edge in garter st, work until armhole measures 8½ (9, 9½, 10, 10)", ending on RS row.

- Beg short-row shaping on next WS row. Work in patt for 9 (10, 12, 12, 14) sts, W and T, work back in patt. Work 4 (5, 6, 6, 7) sts in patt, W and T, work back. Work one more row to retrieve wraps. BO all sts.

Right Front

Buttonhole placement for women; see sidebar at right.

- CO 38 (42, 46, 48, 52) sts. Work in patt st to last 5 sts, PM, K5. Keeping 5 sts at center front in garter st, work until piece measures 6½ (7, 7, 8, 9)", ending with a WS row.

- Work across 13 (15, 15, 16, 17) sts, PM, cont across next 17 (17, 21, 21, 23) sts, PM, finish row. Work 5 (5, 5, 7, 7) rows, keeping sts inside markers in garter st. **Next row (RS):** work to marker, BO sts between markers, cont across row. **Next row:** Work across to bound-off sts, with WS

Making One-Row Buttonholes

Work buttonholes as follows on right front edge for women and on left front edge for men. After 3 (5, 4, 4, 3) ridges have been completed on front edge, work one-row buttonhole so 2 sts rem at front edge: Work to position of buttonhole. Move yarn forward, sl 1 purlwise, move yarn back. *Sl 1 st purlwise from left needle to right needle, pass the second st on right needle over first st, as if to BO. Rep from * 1 more time. Slip the rem stitch from the right needle to the left needle. Turn work, using cable cast on (see right), CO 3 sts. Turn work. Sl first st on left needle over to right needle and pass the extra CO st on right needle over to close buttonhole. Rep buttonhole after 13 (14, 15, 12, 14) ridges as you cont in patt.

Cable cast on: Insert right needle between 2 sts on left needle, wrap yarn around needle as if to knit, pull new loop through to front, place new st on left needle from right side of loop, or by your right thumb, without dropping st off of left needle.

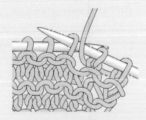

Bring yarn to front.
Slip one stitch purlwise.

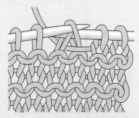

Move yarn to back. Slip another stitch purlwise. Pass first slipped stitch over the second.

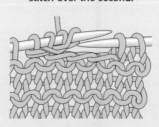

Cast on 3 stitches.

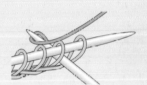

Insert needle between two stitches. Knit a stitch.

Place new stitch on left needle.

of pocket lining facing, place sts on left needle, work across pocket lining keeping cont of patt, finish row. Cont in patt st until piece measures 11 (12½, 13, 14, 15)", ending on WS row.

• **Armhole:** Keeping 13 (13, 15, 15) sts at armhole edge in garter st for 9 rows, work rem sts in patt. BO 9 (9, 9, 11, 11) sts at beg of next WS row—29 (33, 37, 37, 41) sts. Cont in patt until armhole measures 3½ (4, 4½, 4½, 4½)", ending on WS row.

• **Neck:** On next RS row, K21 (23, 24, 24, 25) sts, PM, work rem of row in patt as established. Keeping 21 (23, 24, 24, 25) sts in garter st, work 6 more rows. BO 16 (18, 19, 19, 20) sts at neck edge—13 (15, 18, 18, 21) sts. Keeping 5 sts at neck edge in garter st, cont until armhole measures 8½ (9, 9½, 10, 10)", ending on WS row.

• Beg short-row shaping on next RS row. Work in patt for 9 (10, 12, 12, 14) sts, W and T, work back in patt. Work 4 (5, 6, 6, 7) sts in patt, W and T, work back. Work one more row to retrieve wraps. BO all sts.

Finishing

• Weave shoulder and side seams tog.

• Mist and lay flat to dry, smoothing with hand.

• Sew on buttons to appropriate front.

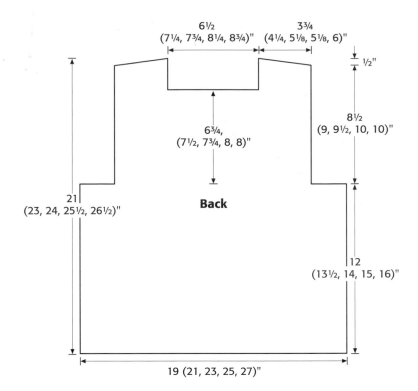

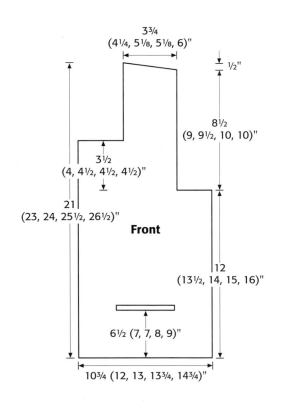

Columbus

Work this striped, ribbed sweater in many colors or the three listed.

It's a great way to use scraps to make a wonderful vest for men and women.

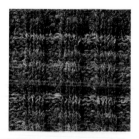

Skill Level: Intermediate

Sizes: Small (Medium, Large, X-Large, XX-Large)

Finished Chest: 33 (39, 46, 52, 55½)"

Finished Length: 21 (22½, 24, 25½, 28)"

Materials

(A) 4 (5, 6, 7, 8) skeins Chelsea Silk from Tahki/Stacy Charles (65% silk, 35% wool; 105 yds, 50 g per skein), color 122A, or other worsted weight yarn

(B) 2 (3, 4, 5, 6) skeins Champion from Skacel (54% wool, 10% synthetic, 36% nylon; 54 yds, 50 g per skein), color 2, or other bulky weight yarn

(C) 2 (3, 3, 4, 5) skeins Aquarius from Trendsetter (78% nylon, 22% cotton; 96 yds, 50 g per skein), color 812, or other worsted weight yarn

24" size 7 circular needles

Size 8 needles (or size required to obtain gauge)

4 stitch holders

1 ring marker

Gauge

15 sts and 20 rows = 4" in pattern stitch on size 8 needles

Pattern Stitch

Multiple of 6 + 8.

Rows 1 and 2: P4, (K3, P3) across, end K4.

Rep rows 1 and 2.

Color Sequence

3 rows color C

2 rows color B

1 row color C

2 rows color A

2 rows color C

3 rows color A

2 rows color B

1 row color A

Note: Rep the 2 rows of patt st in the above color sequence, changing colors as directed. Carry yarns not in use loosely up the side; twist together with yarn in use to keep yarn floats up the sides from being too long. You will know you have made a mistake if the yarn you are to use next is not waiting for you to work the row and color sequence you are to work next. Yarns will have to be cut and restarted after armhole bind off.

Back

• *With size 8 needles and color A, CO 62 (74, 86, 98, 104) sts, work patt st for 3 rows, then beg color sequence in patt st until piece measures 12 (13, 14, 15, 17)" *.

• **Armhole:** Keeping continuity of patt, BO 6 (7, 8, 9, 9) sts at beg of next 2 rows, dec 3 (5, 6, 7, 7) sts at each end EOR—44 (50, 58, 66, 72) sts. Cont until armhole measures 8 (8½, 9, 9½, 10).

• **Back neck:** Work across 13 (15, 17, 19, 21) sts, BO 18 (20, 24, 28, 30) sts, cont across rem 13 (15, 17, 19, 21) sts.

• **Left shoulder:** Dec 1 st at neck edge EOR 2 times. Cont until armhole measures 9 (9½, 10, 10½, 11)", place 11 (13, 15, 17, 19) sts on stitch holder.

• **Right shoulder:** Rejoin yarn to right shoulder sts with WS facing and work as for left shoulder, reversing shaping and maintaining patt and color sequence.

Front

• Work from * to * of back. Work across 31 (37, 43, 49, 52) sts, leave rem 31 (37, 43, 49, 52) sts on knitting needle or a large holder.

• **Left Armhole and V neck:** Keeping continuity of patt, BO 6 (7, 8, 9, 9) sts at beg of next row. Dec 1 st EOR at armhole edge 3 (5, 6, 7, 7) times, and *at same time* dec 1 st at neck edge every fourth row 7 (7, 8, 8, 8) times, then EOR 4 (5, 6, 8, 9) times—11 (13, 15, 17, 19) sts. Cont until armhole measures 9 (9½, 10, 10½, 11)". Place sts on stitch holder.

• **Right Armhole and V neck:** Rejoin yarn at V neck and work as for left armhole and V neck, reversing shaping.

Finishing

• Work 3-needle BO for shoulders.

• Weave side seams tog.

• **Neckband:** With size 7 needles and color A, starting at right shoulder seam, PU 5 (7, 6,

6, 8) sts, 17 (19, 21, 27, 29) sts across bound-off sts of back neck, 5 (7, 6, 6, 8) sts to left shoulder seam, 39 (39, 45, 45, 51) sts to center front, PM, 1 st at center front, 39 (39, 45, 45, 51) sts to right shoulder seam, PM—106 (112, 124, 130, 148) sts. Working in the round, work K3, P3 ribbing to marker, K1, (P3, K3) around to last 3 sts, P3. **Next 2 rounds:** work in patt to 2 sts from center front, P2tog, K1, SSP, patt to end. **Next round:** BO to center front 3 sts, slip next 2 sts tog as if to knit,

P1, P2SSO. Cont to BO to end. Finish off.

• **Armhole bands:** With size 7 needles and color A, starting at underarm seam, PU 6 (8, 7, 8, 8) sts across bound off sts, 6 (8, 10, 12, 12) sts on dec edge, 36 (38, 43, 46, 46) sts to shoulder, rep in reverse for other side, PM— 96 (108, 120, 132, 132) sts. Working in the round, work P3, K3 for 3 rounds. BO loosely.

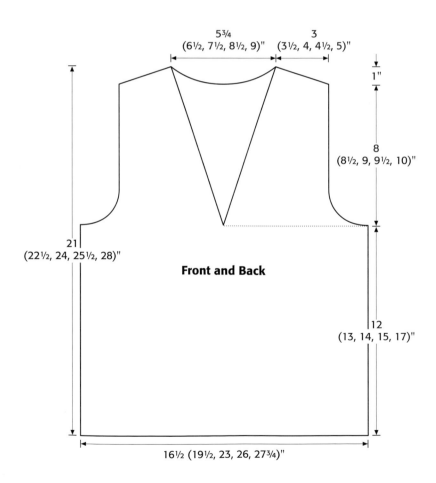

5¾
(6½, 7½, 8½, 9)"   3
                    (3½, 4, 4½, 5)"

1"

8
(8½, 9, 9½, 10)"

21
(22½, 24, 25½, 28)"

Front and Back

12
(13, 14, 15, 17)"

16½ (19½, 23, 26, 27¾)"

Dallas

The wonderful blend of fibers in this yarn make the mitered hems and borders in this garment a wonderful alternative to ribbing. The rayon in this yarn will allow you to steam and press the borders firmly enough to make them lie flat. Be sure if you are substituting yarns that the new yarn will tolerate the amount of steam and pressing it takes to make the borders lie flat. Do not use acrylic or nylon yarn.

Skill Level: Intermediate

Sizes: Small (Medium, Large, X-Large, XX-Large)

Finished Chest: 36 (40, 44, 48, 52)"

Finished Length: 22 (24, 25, 26½, 27)"

Materials

Soft Twist from Berroco (42% wool, 59% rayon; 100 yds, 50 g per skein) in the following amounts and colors:

   MC 5 (6, 8, 9, 10) skeins color 9450, or other light worsted weight yarn

   CC 3 (4, 5, 6, 7) skeins color 9420, or other light worsted weight yarn

Size 7 needles (or size required to obtain gauge)

24" size 4 circular needles for borders

24" size 5 circular needles for borders

4 stitch holders

Small amount of cotton yarn in contrasting color for provisional cast on

Size G crochet hook

Three 2" clasps

Gauge

20 sts and 28 rows = 4" in stockinette st on size 7 needles after steaming

Right Front

• Work from ** to ** of left front. Work 9 rows in St st as given for back except at beg of knit rows, K1, M1, K to end. When 9 rows have been completed, change to size 5 needle and reverse shaping at beg of knit rows by working SSK. Finish as for back hem. Cont in St st in MC until piece measures 13 (14, 15, 16, 16)" from bottom of hem, ending on RS row.

• **Armhole:** BO 13 (15, 18, 20, 22) sts at beg of next WS row. At same time, dec 1 st at neck edge every fourth row 11 (12, 13, 15, 17) times—16 (18, 19, 20, 21) sts. Work until armhole measures 8½ (9½, 9½, 10, 10½)", end on WS row.

• Work short-row shaping as for back left shoulder. Place sts on stitch holder.

Finishing

• Work 3-needle BO for shoulders.

• Weave side seams tog.

Note: The borders are knit in sections with mitered edges. The pieces are then woven together to create the mitered corners. When weaving pieces together, weave underside of hem first and then the side of the border on front of garment. These are awkward seams because of the mitered edges.

• **Lower armhole band:** *With size 5 needle, PU 23 (30, 36, 40, 44) sts across lower edge of armhole with RS facing. Be sure to PU a st in the corners. Work 9 rows of St st starting with a purl row and *at same time* on RS rows, work a SSK at beg of row, and K2tog at end of row. Next WS row, change to size 4 needle and purl across. Work 8 more rows, on RS rows M1 at each end. BO in purl*.

• **Upper armhole band:** Work from * to * of lower armhole band, except PU 49 (55, 55, 59, 64) sts on each side of shoulder seam—98 (110, 110, 118, 128) sts.

• **Back neckband:** Work from * to * of lower armhole band, except PU 32 (34, 36, 40, 44) sts across bound-off sts of back neck.

• **Left front band:** With RS facing and size 5 needle, starting at back neck, PU 10 (10, 10, 10, 10) sts from back neck to shoulder seam, 50 (55, 55, 59, 64) sts to start of V-neck shaping, and 58 (65, 72, 79, 86) sts to end of front—118 (130, 137, 148, 160) sts. Work 9 rows in St st starting with a purl row. On RS rows, work a SSK at beg of row, and K2tog at end of row. Change to size 4 needle, purl 1 row. Work 8 more rows in St st. On RS rows, M1 at each end. BO in purl.

• **Right front band:** Work as for left front band, except pick up sts starting at lower-right front.

• Weave all mitered corners tog.

• Whipstitch the BO sts of the bands to the CC purl bars that remain from picking up sts. Be careful to make the sewing loose enough that the borders remain elastic.

• Heat an iron so that it is very steamy. Lay the vest on an ironing board with WS facing and beg steaming all of the borders on WS. Be careful to keep all of the matching edges the same size. Steam again on RS. Gently steam the body to the correct measurements. Leave flat to dry.

• Sew the first clasp at the beg of V-neck shaping and sew the next 2 below the first one, 2" apart.

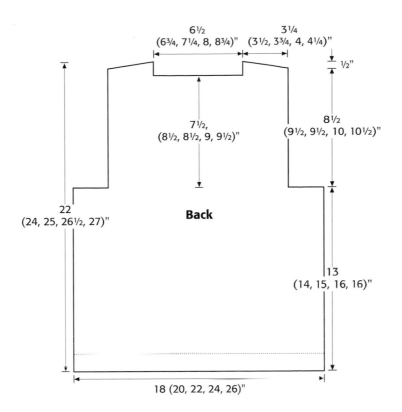

6½
(6¾, 7¼, 8, 8¾)"

3¼
(3½, 3¾, 4, 4¼)"

½"

7½,
(8½, 8½, 9, 9½)"

8½
(9½, 9½, 10, 10½)"

22
(24, 25, 26½, 27)"

Back

13
(14, 15, 16, 16)"

18 (20, 22, 24, 26)"

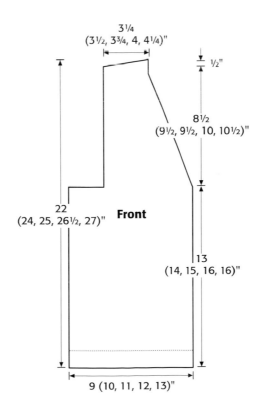

3¼
(3½, 3¾, 4, 4¼)"

½"

8½
(9½, 9½, 10, 10½)"

22
(24, 25, 26½, 27)"

Front

13
(14, 15, 16, 16)"

9 (10, 11, 12, 13)"

Anchorage

This is a simple slip-stitch pattern with a twist. Note that the extra colors in the stripes made with the wool and chenille yarn are worked for part or all of a row. This vest for men and women can be easily worked in two colors instead of four if desired.

Skill Level: Intermediate

Sizes: Small (Medium, Large, X-Large, XX-Large)

Finished Chest: 36 (40, 43, 46, 50)"

Finished Length: 20½ (22, 23½, 25, 26½)"

Materials

Highland Style Wool from Harrisville Yarns (100% wool; 200 yds, 100 g per skein) in the following amounts and colors:

(A) 2 (2, 3, 3, 4) skeins Peacock, or other worsted weight yarn

(B) 2 (2, 3, 3, 4) skeins Tundra, or other worsted weight yarn

Jasmine from Harrisville Yarns (100% virgin wool twisted with 100% rayon chenille) in the following amounts and colors:

(C) 1 skein Sweet Olive, or other worsted weight yarn

(D) 1 skein Angel's Trumpet, or other worsted weight yarn

Size 6 needles

Size 8 needles (or size required to obtain gauge)

2 ring markers

1 safety pin

Gauge

18 sts and 32 rows = 4" in pattern stitch on size 8 needles

Pattern Stitch

Multiple of 4 + 5.

Note: If you are using 2 colors instead of 4, work the 4-row patt below using colors A and B.

Row 1 (RS): With color A, K4, *sl 1 wyib, K3, rep from * to last st, end K1.

Row 2: With color A, K4, *sl 1 wyif, K3, rep from * to last st, end K1.

Row 3: With color B, K2, *sl 1 wyib, K3, rep from * to last 3 sts, end sl 1 wyib, K2.

Row 4: With color B, K2, *sl 1, wyif, K3, rep from * to last 3 sts, end sl 1 wyif, K2.

Rep rows 1–4 for patt st.

Note: For colors C and D you will need to cut yarn and move to the row where it is to be used next.

**After 4 reps of patt st, on next rep: Substitute color C for B.

Work 4 reps of patt st, on fifth rep, rows 1 and 2: Substitute color D for A for first 52 sts only. On next row, work color A sts in color A and color D sts in color D, twisting colors where they join to close gap.

Work 4 reps of patt st, on fifth rep, rows 3 and 4: Substitute color C for color B on last 58 sts only by working to 58 sts from the end with color C, change to color B for rem sts. On row 4, work color C sts in color C and color B sts in color B, twisting colors where they join to close gap.

Work 4 reps of patt st, on fifth rep, rows 1 and 2: Substitute color D for color A.

Work 4 reps of patt st, on fifth rep, rows 3 and 4: Substitute color C for color B for first 35 sts, rejoin color B for rest of row. On row 4, work color B sts in color B and color C sts in color C, twisting colors where they join to close gap.

Work 4 reps of patt st: Substitute D for A on last 47 sts, twisting colors where they join to close gap.

Rep from **.

Back

• With size 6 needles and color A, CO 75 (83, 91, 99, 107) sts. Knit 3 rows. Change to color B, knit 2 rows, inc 6 sts on last row—81 (89, 97, 105, 113) sts. Change to size 8 needles and beg patt st and color placement. Cont in patt until piece measures 12 (13, 14, 15, 16)".

• **Armholes:** BO 12 (12, 12, 16, 16) sts at beg of next 2 rows— 57 (65, 73, 73, 81) sts. Cont in patt until armhole measures 8 (8½, 9, 9½, 10)".

• **Left shoulder:** Work across 13 (16, 19, 19, 21) sts in patt. Leave rem 44 (49, 54, 54, 60) sts on left needle. Work next 4 rows of patt. BO all sts.

• **Back neck and right shoulder:** Reattach yarn in correct color sequence to neck edge with RS facing. BO 31 (33, 35, 35, 39) sts, work across rem 13 (16, 19, 19, 21) sts. Work 3 more rows, BO all sts.

Front

• Work as for back to armholes. BO for armholes and *at same time*, place center st on a safety pin.

• **Left front:** Cont in patt on first 28 (32, 36, 36, 40) sts. Keeping edge st at neck edge in garter st, work a dec one st in from neck edge on every row 1 of patt st until 13 (16, 19, 19, 21) sts rem. Cont until armhole measures 8½ (9, 9½, 10, 10½)". BO all sts.

• **Right front:** Reattach yarn in correct color sequence and work as for left front, reversing shaping. Don't forget color placement rows that affect only the right front.

Finishing

• Weave shoulder and side seams tog.

• Be sure to close the gaps, if necessary, where color changes occurred in the middle of a row as you weave in the ends.

• **Neckband:** With size 6 needles and color B, starting at right shoulder seam, PU 34 (36, 38, 40, 42) sts to left shoulder seam, 34 (36, 38, 40, 42) sts to center front, PM, knit the st on the pin, PU 34 (36, 38, 40, 42)

sts to right shoulder seam, PM—102 (108, 114, 120, 126) sts. Working in the round, purl 1 round. Change to color A, *knit to 2 sts before marker, K2tog, slip marker, K1, K2tog, knit to end. Purl 1 round*. Rep from * to * once. BO all sts in purl.

• **Armhole bands:** With size 6 needles and color B, starting at underarm seam, PU 12 (12, 12, 16, 16) sts across bound-off sts,

34 (37, 41, 45, 49) sts to shoulder seam, rep in reverse for other side. PM—92 (98, 106, 122, 130) sts. Working in the round, purl 1 round. Change to color A, knit 1 round, BO all sts in purl.

• Lay flat and mist with water; smooth with your hands. Do not steam or press the vest; the texture of the patt should stand out.

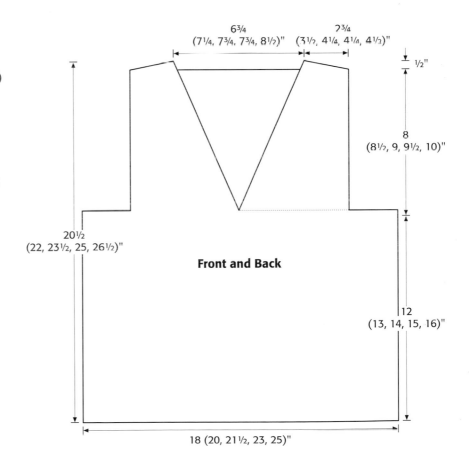

Puget Sound

Mohair and wool knit around the body instead of up and down create this vest with off-center button closure. I love the way the two yarns in the same colorway interplay with each other.

Skill Level: Intermediate

Sizes: Small (Medium, Large, X-Large, XX-Large)

Finished Chest: 36 (40, 44, 48, 52)"

Finished Length: 22½ (23½, 24½, 25½, 26½)"

Materials

MC 2 (2, 3, 3, 3) skeins 4/8's Wool from Mountain Colors (100% wool; 250 yds, 100 g per skein), color Silverbow, or other worsted weight yarn

CC 2 (2, 3, 3, 4) skeins Mohair from Mountain Colors (78% mohair, 13% wool, 9% nylon; 225 yds, 100 g per skein), color Silverbow, or other mohair bulky weight yarn

24" size 7 circular needles

Size 8 needles

Size 10 needles (or size required to obtain gauge)

5 buttons, ¾" diameter

2 ring markers

Gauge

15 sts and 18 rows = 4" in pattern stitch on size 10 needles

Pattern Stitch

Rows 1–6: With MC, work in St st.

Rows 7–10: With CC, knit every row.

Rep rows 1–10.

Vest

• **Right front:** With size 8 needles and CC, CO 70 (74, 76, 78, 82) sts. Knit 3 rows.

• **Buttonhole row:** K9 (9, 10, 11, 12), YO, K2tog, *K6 (7, 8, 9, 10), YO, K2tog, rep from * 3 more times, work to end of row. Cont in garter st for 5 more rows ending with a WS row. Change to size 10 needles and MC, beg patt st and work until front measures 6 (6½, 7, 7½, 8)".

• **Right neck and shoulder:** CO 14 (14, 16, 18, 18) sts at neck edge, cont in patt until shoulder measures 4¼ (5, 5½, 6¼, 6½)".

• **Right armhole:** *BO 34 (38, 38, 40, 44) sts at shoulder edge. Cont in patt until side measures 3½ (3½, 4, 4, 5)" from cast-off area of armhole.

• **Back:** CO 34 (38, 38, 40, 44) sts at armhole edge*. Cont in patt until back measures 14½ (16½, 18, 20, 21)".

• **Left armhole:** Work from * to * of right armhole and back.

• **Left front:** Cont in patt, when shoulder measures 4¼ (5, 5½, 6¼, 6½)" change to size 8 needles and CC, knit 9 rows. BO sts loosely.

Finishing

• Sew shoulder seams, including front left band to back neck.

• **Armhole bands:** With size 7 needles, CC, and RS facing, start at middle of underarm, PU 7 (8, 9, 9, 10) sts to corner, 33 (37, 37, 39, 43) sts to shoulder seam and rep in reverse for other side, PM—80 (90, 92, 96, 106) sts. Working in the round, (purl 1 row, knit 1 row) 3 times, knit 1 more round. BO sts loosely in purl.

• **Neckband:** With size 7 needles and CC, starting at right front border edge, PU 5 sts across top of garter st border, 28 (30, 32, 34, 36) sts to corner, PM, PU 14 (15, 16, 18, 18) sts to next corner, PM, PU 22 (24, 26, 28, 31) sts across back—69 (74, 79, 85, 90) sts. Knit 8 rows, and *at same time* on RS rows 2 and 4, at both markers, knit to 2 sts from marker, K2tog, slip marker, SSK. *At same time*, at beg of row 4, place buttonhole as follows: K3, YO, K2tog. BO on row 9. Sew neckband to bound-off edge of front left band.

• Lay out flat and pin to measurements. Mist with water and let dry completely.

• Sew on buttons.

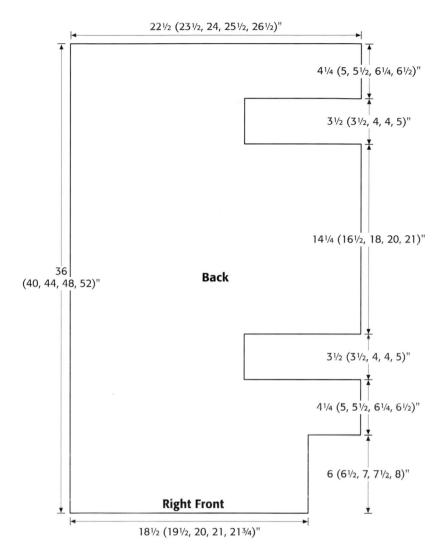

22½ (23½, 24, 25½, 26½)"

4¼ (5, 5½, 6¼, 6½)"

3½ (3½, 4, 4, 5)"

14¼ (16½, 18, 20, 21)"

36 (40, 44, 48, 52)"

Back

3½ (3½, 4, 4, 5)"

4¼ (5, 5½, 6¼, 6½)"

6 (6½, 7, 7½, 8)"

Right Front

18½ (19½, 20, 21, 21¾)"

Atlanta

The subtle shading of this yarn creates a beautiful background for the cables and basket-weave stitch in this pattern. Worked in any color you choose, this vest is great for both men and women.

Skill Level: Intermediate

Sizes: Small (Medium, Large, X-Large)

Finished Chest: 34½ (41, 47, 53)"

Finished Length: 20½ (22, 23½, 25)"

Materials

4 (4, 5, 6) skeins Lamb's Pride Superwash from Brown Sheep (100% wool; 200 yds, 100 g per skein), color SW55 Plum Crazy, or other worsted weight yarn

24" size 5 circular needles

Size 7 needles (or size required to obtain gauge)

Cable needle

1 safety pin

2 ring markers

Stitch holder

Gauge

20 sts and 32 rows = 4" in pattern stitch on size 7 needles

Pattern Stitch

Multiple of 8 + 6.

Note: Directions include one st at each edge that is worked in garter st throughout.

C4F: Cable worked over 4 sts. Sl 2 sts to cn and hold in front of work. K2 from knitting needle, K2 from cn.

Rows 1 and 3 (WS): K1, *P4, K4, rep from * to last 5 sts, end P4, K1.

Row 2: K1, *K4, P4, rep from * to last 5 sts, end K5.

Row 4: K1, *P4, K4, C4F, K4, rep from * to last 5 sts, end P4, K1.

Rows 5 and 7: K1, *K4, P12, rep from * to last 5 sts, end K4, P1.

Row 6: K1, *P4, K12, rep from * to last 5 sts, end P4, K1.

Row 8: K1, *K4, P4, C4F, P4, rep from * to last 5 sts, end K4, P1.

Rows 9 and 11: K1, *P4, K4, rep from * to last 5 sts, end P4, K1.

Row 10: K1, *K4, P4, rep from * to last 5 sts, end K4, P1.

Rep rows 4–11.

Back

- With size 7 needles, CO 86 (102, 118, 134) sts. Beg patt st and work until piece measures 12 (13, 14, 15)".

- **Armholes:** Keeping continuity of patt, BO 8 (8, 10, 14) sts at beg of next 2 rows, dec 1 st at each end EOR 4 (4, 5, 8) times—62 (78, 88, 90) sts. Cont in patt until armhole measures 8 (8½, 9, 9½)", ending on WS row.

- **Right shoulder and back neck:** Work across 16 (21, 24, 25) sts, leave rem 46 (57, 64, 65) sts on needle, turn and work WS row. Dec 1 st at neck edge every row 2 (3, 3, 3) times—14 (18, 21, 22) sts. BO all sts in patt.

- **Left shoulder and back neck:** Reattach yarn at neck edge with RS facing, BO center 30 (36, 40, 40) sts. Work as for right shoulder, reversing shaping.

Front

- Work as for back until piece measures 12 (13, 14, 15)". Beg armhole shaping and *at same time* beg V-neck shaping: Work to center 2 sts and place on safety pin. Place rem sts for right front on stitch holder or leave on knitting needle.

- **Left front:** On next RS row, dec 1 st at neck edge EOR 16 (20, 22, 22) times—14 (18, 21, 22) sts. Work until armhole measures 8½ (9, 9½, 10)". BO all sts on same row as shoulders for back.

- **Right front:** Reattach yarn at center front and work as for left front, reversing shaping.

Finishing

• Weave shoulder and side seams together.

• **Neckband:** With size 5 needles, starting at right shoulder seam, PU 4 (5, 6, 7) sts to back neck, 30 (36, 42, 40) sts across bound-off sts of back neck, 4 (5, 6, 7) sts to left shoulder seam, 46 (50, 50, 54) sts to center front, knit 2 sts on safety pin, PM between 2 sts, PU 46 (50, 50, 54) sts to right shoulder seam, PM—132 (148, 156, 164) sts. Working in the round, work in K2, P2 ribbing for 1 round. **Next 4 rounds:** Work in ribbing to 2 sts before center front marker, SSK, slip marker, K2tog, rib to end of round. BO all sts in patt.

• **Armhole bands:** With size 5 needles, starting at underarm seam, PU 7 (7, 9, 14) sts across bound-off sts, 7 (7, 9, 14) sts on dec section, 34 (36, 38, 42) sts to shoulder seam, rep in reverse for other side, PM—96 (100, 112, 140) sts. Working in the round, work in K2, P2 ribbing for 5 rounds. BO all sts in patt.

• Pin out to correct measurements, mist with water, and smooth with your hand. Allow to dry before removing. You may need to rep process for opposite side. Do not steam or press. The pattern texture should stand out.

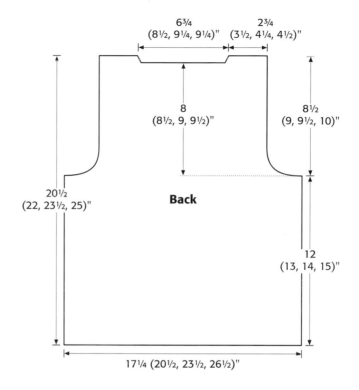

6¾ (8½, 9¼, 9¼)"   2¾ (3½, 4¼, 4½)"

8 (8½, 9, 9½)"   8½ (9, 9½, 10)"

20½ (22, 23½, 25)"

Back

12 (13, 14, 15)"

17¼ (20½, 23½, 26½)"

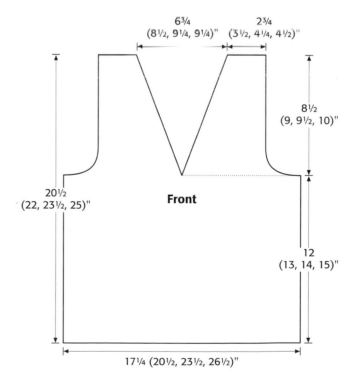

6¾ (8½, 9¼, 9¼)"   2¾ (3½, 4¼, 4½)"

8½ (9, 9½, 10)"

20½ (22, 23½, 25)"

Front

12 (13, 14, 15)"

17¼ (20½, 23½, 26½)"

Portland

The bobbles in the border and the unusual rib patt in wonderful cotton yarn

make a vest for the office or for play. I love it in red.

Skill Level: Intermediate

Sizes: Small (Medium, Large, X-Large, XX-Large)

Finished Chest: 36 (40, 44, 48, 52)"

Finished Length: 21 (22, 23, 24, 25½)"

Materials

3 (4, 5, 6, 6) skeins Provence from Classic Elite (100% mercerized cotton; 256 yds, 125 g per skein), color 2267, or other DK weight yarn

24" size 5 circular needles

Size 6 needles (or size required to obtain gauge)

4 stitch holders

1 safety pin

2 ring markers

Gauge

20 sts and 28 rows = 4" in pattern on size 6 needles

Back

• With size 5 needles, CO 91 (101, 111, 121, 131) sts. Work border as follows:

• **Row 1 (WS):** K5, *P1, K9, rep from *, end last rep with K5 instead of K9.

• **Row 2 (RS):** K5, *(K1, P1) twice in next st, (turn, K4) 3 times, turn. Lift second, third, and fourth st in that order over the first st on left needle, knit the one rem st, K9, rep from *, end last rep with K5 instead of K9.

• **Row 3:** K5, *P1, K4, rep from *, end last rep with K5 instead of K4.

• **Row 4:** K1, *YO, K2, SSK, K1, K2tog, K2, YO, K1, rep from * to end.

• **Row 5:** P2, K3, *P1, K3, P3, K3, rep from *, work last rep as P1, K3, P2.

• **Row 6:** K2, *YO, K1, SSK, K1, K2tog, K1, YO, K3, rep from *, end last rep with K2 instead of K3.

• **Row 7:** P3, K2, *P1, K2, P5, K2, rep from *, work last rep as P1, K2, P3.

• **Row 8:** K3, *YO, SSK, K1, K2tog, YO, K5, rep from *, end last rep with K3 instead of K5.

• **Row 9:** P4, *K1, P1, K1, P7, rep from *, end last rep with P4 instead of P7.

• **Row 10:** Knit.

Change to size 6 needles and rep rows 9 and 10 until piece measures 13 (13½, 14, 14½, 15)" from bottom of hem.

• **Armholes:** BO 10 (11, 12, 12, 13) sts at beg of next 2 rows**. Dec 1 st at each end EOR 3 (4, 4, 5, 6) times—65 (71, 79, 87, 93) sts. Cont until armhole measures 8 (8½, 9, 9½, 10½)", ending with a WS row.

• **Neck and shoulders:** Work across 15 (17, 19, 21, 23) sts, place on stitch holder. BO center 35 (37, 41, 45, 47) sts, cont across rem 15 (17, 19, 21, 23) sts, place on stitch holder.

Front

• Work as for back to **. On next RS row, work across 35 (39, 43, 48, 52) sts, place center st on safety pin. Place rem 35 (39, 43, 48, 52) sts on large holder or leave on knitting needle.

• **Left front:** Cont in patt, dec 1 st at beg of EOR 3 (4, 4, 5, 6) times, and *at same time* dec 1 st EOR at neck edge until 15 (17, 19, 21, 23) sts rem. Cont until armhole measures 8 (8½, 9, 9½, 10½)", place on stitch holder.

• **Right front:** Leave center st on safety pin. Place rem sts back on knitting needle and work as for left front, reversing shaping.

Finishing

• Work 3-needle BO for shoulders.

• Weave side seams tog.

• **Neckband:** With size 5 needles, starting at right shoulder seam, PU 35 (37, 41, 45, 47) sts across back neck to left shoulder seam, 50 (56, 58, 60, 64) sts to center st on pin, knit 1 st from pin, PM, PU 50 (56, 58, 60, 64) sts to right shoulder seam, PM—136 (150, 158, 166, 176) sts. Working in the round, **round 1:** Purl to st before marker, K1, purl to end. **Round 2:** Knit to 2 sts from marker, K2tog, slip marker, K1, K2tog, knit to end of row. Rep rounds 1 and 2 once. BO loosely in purl.

• **Armhole bands:** With size 5 needles, starting at underarm seam, PU 10 (11, 12, 12, 13) sts across bound-off sts, 4 (6, 6, 8, 10) sts on dec edge, 42 (44, 46, 48, 52) sts on straight edge, 1 st at shoulder seam, rep in reverse for other side, excluding 1 st at shoulder seam—113 (123, 129, 137, 151) sts. Working in the round, (purl 1 round, knit 1 round) twice. BO loosely in purl.

• Moisten and lay flat to dry.

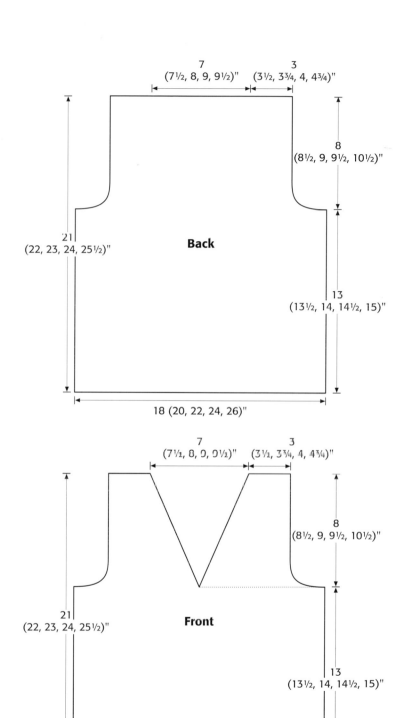

San Diego

A very simple lace pattern makes this a wonderful vest for any time of the year.

The front borders, including the buttonholes, are knit at the same time as the body.

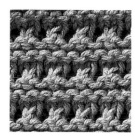

Skill Level: Intermediate

Sizes: Small (Medium, Large, X-Large, XX-Large)

Finished Chest: 37 (41, 45, 49, 53)"

Finished Length: 23 (23½, 24, 25, 26)"

Materials

4 (4, 5, 6, 7) skeins Sierra from Cascade Yarns (80% Pima cotton, 20% wool; 191 yds, 100 g per skein), color 23, or other worsted weight yarn

24" size 5 circular needles

24" size 6 circular needles (or size required to obtain gauge)

5 buttons, ¾" diameter

4 stitch holders

1 ring marker

Gauge

16 sts and 32 rows = 4" in pattern stitch on size 6 needles

Pattern Stitch

Multiple of 2 + 2.

Row 1: K1, (YO, K2tog) to last st, K1.

Row 2: Purl.

Rows 3–6: Knit.

Rep these 6 rows for patt.

Back

• With size 5 needles, CO 74 (82, 90, 98, 106) sts. Knit 7 (7, 7, 9, 9) rows. Change to size 6 needles, work in patt until piece measures 13½ (14, 14, 15, 16)".

• **Armholes:** Keeping continuity of patt, BO 7 (8, 9, 9, 10) sts at beg of next 2 rows, dec 1 st at each end EOR 4 (5, 5, 5, 6) times—52 (56, 62, 70, 74) sts. Work until armhole measures 8½ (8½, 9, 9, 10)".

• **Right shoulder:** Work across 16 (16, 17, 21, 22) sts, turn, cont in patt, leave rem sts on needle. Dec 1 st at neck edge on next

RS row—15 (15, 16, 20, 21) sts. When armhole measures 9½ (9½, 10, 10, 11)", place sts on stitch holder.

• **Left shoulder:** Reattach yarn at neck edge with RS facing, BO center 20 (24, 28, 28, 30) sts, cont across rem 16 (16, 17, 21, 22) sts. Work 1 dec at neck edge on next RS row, and finish as for right shoulder.

Left Front

• Work as for back except CO 42 (46, 50, 54, 58) sts. Keeping 5 (5, 5, 5, 5) sts in garter st at center front edge (PM to designate 5 sts), work until side seam measures 13½ (14, 14, 15, 16)". Count patt rows to be sure they match the back side seam.

• **Armhole and V neck:** BO 7 (8, 9, 9, 10) sts at armhole edge. Dec 1 st at armhole edge EOR 4 (5, 5, 5, 6) times and *at same time*, dec 1 st at neck edge on body side of border every fourth row 16 (18, 20, 20, 21) times— 15 (15, 16, 20, 21) sts.

• When armhole measures 9½ (9½, 10, 10, 11)", place 15 (15, 16, 20, 21) shoulder sts on a holder. Cont with 5 sts for neck border in garter st as follows: CO 1 st at inside edge and cont on 6 sts until border fits around neck to center back when slightly stretched. BO on next WS row.

Right Front

Note: there will be no K1 at the end of row 1 for the right front only.

• CO 42 (46, 50, 54, 58) sts, work as for left front, keeping 5 sts at center front in garter st and placing buttonholes as follows: At beg of RS row, K2, YO, K2tog, K1, cont across row in patt st. Work first buttonhole after bottom border is com-pleted, then after every 12 (12, 12, 13, 14) garter st ridges for a total of 5 buttonholes.

• Work as for left front, reversing shaping.

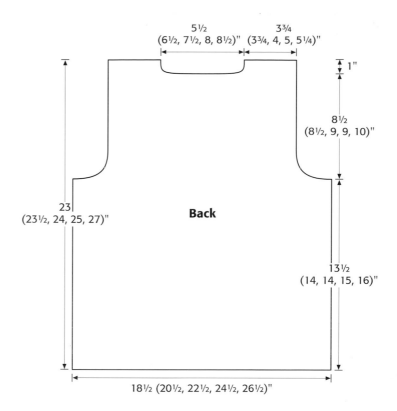

5½
(6½, 7½, 8, 8½)"   3¾ (3¾, 4, 5, 5¼)"

1"

8½
(8½, 9, 9, 10)"

23
(23½, 24, 25, 27)"

Back

13½
(14, 14, 15, 16)"

18½ (20½, 22½, 24½, 26½)"

Finishing

• Work 3-needle BO for shoulders.

• Weave neck border sts tog and weave to back neck.

• Weave side seams tog.

• **Armhole bands:** With size 5 needles and RS facing, starting at underarm, PU 7 (8, 9, 9, 10) sts across bound-off sts, 53 (53, 55, 55, 59) sts to shoulder seam, 1 st at shoulder seam, and rep in reverse for other side of armhole, excluding 1 st at shoulder seam, PM—121 (123, 129, 129, 139) sts. Working in the round, (knit 1 row, purl 1 row) 2 (2, 2, 3, 3) times. BO in purl.

• Pin borders and seams, stretching slightly to help them lie flat. Mist with water and smooth with hand to block gently. Leave flat until dry.

• Sew on buttons.

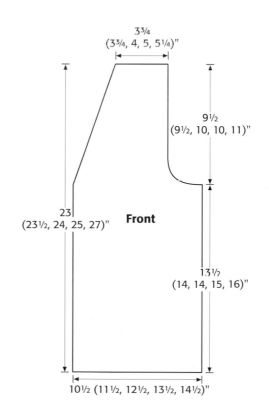

3¾
(3¾, 4, 5, 5¼)"

9½
(9½, 10, 10, 11)"

23
(23½, 24, 25, 27)"   **Front**

13½
(14, 14, 15, 16)"

10½ (11½, 12½, 13½, 14½)"

Whidbey Island

This heavyweight vest for men and women is perfect for an adventure outdoors or some extra warmth indoors. It is easy to wear and easy to knit.

Skill Level: Intermediate
Sizes: Small (Medium, Large, X-Large, XX-Large)
Finished Chest: 41 (45¾, 50, 53¼, 56)"
Finished Length: 23 (24½, 26, 27½, 28)"

Materials

5 (5, 6, 7, 8) skeins 100% Shetland Wool from Jamieson (100% wool; 126 yds, 100 g per skein), color Merlot, or other bulky weight yarn

1 skein 2 ply 100% Shetland Wool from Jamieson (100% wool; 150 yds, 25 g per skein), color 235-Grouse for pockets, or other fingering weight yarn

24" size 4 circular needles for pockets only

24" size 8 circular needles

24" size 10 circular needles (or size required to obtain gauge)

Jacket or parka separating zipper to match length of front of vest when completed. If you cannot find a zipper the exact length, it can be cut to the correct measurement. See finishing on page 76.

Small amount of contrasting sewing thread, matching sewing thread, and white size 10 cotton crochet thread

Sewing needle

4 stitch holders

1 ring marker

Gauge

14 sts and 20 rows = 4" in pattern stitch on size 10 needles

Pattern

*With size 10 needles, work 30 rows in St st. Change to size 8 needles, knit 4 rows (2 ridges of garter st). Rep from *.

Back

• With size 8 needles, CO 68 (76, 84, 90, 96) sts. Knit 11 (11, 11, 13, 13) rows. Change to size 10 needles, work in patt until piece measures 14 (15, 16, 17, 17)".

• **Armhole:** BO 8 (8, 8, 9, 9) sts at beg of next 2 rows. Dec 1 st at each end EOR 4 (4, 4, 5, 5) times—44 (52, 60, 62, 68) sts. Cont in patt until armhole measures 8 (8½, 9, 9½, 10)", ending on WS row.

• Beg short-row shaping on next RS row. Knit across to 3 (4, 7, 7, 8) sts from end, W and T, purl to 3 (4, 7, 7, 8) sts from end, W and T, knit to 8 (9, 10, 10, 11) sts from end, W and T, purl to 8 (9, 10, 10, 11) sts from end, W and T. Knit to end of row to retrieve wraps. Turn, purl to end of row, BO center 22 (26, 26, 28, 30) sts, cont purling across row to retrieve wraps. Place 11 (13, 17, 17, 19) sts on stitch holder for each shoulder.

Left Front

• With size 8 needles, CO 38 (42, 46, 48, 50) sts (includes 4 extra sts for front border). Knit 11 (11, 11, 13, 13) rows. Change

to size 10 needles. Keeping center front 4 sts in garter st, work in patt as for back to end of first garter st section.

• **Divide for pocket:** Cont in patt, working on first 10 (14, 16, 16, 18) sts only, leave rem sts to be worked later. CO 2 sts at inside edge of pocket and work the 30 rows of St st, on last row BO 2 sts at pocket edge. Place sts on stitch holder. Work rem sts that have been on hold in patt to same row. To join 2 pieces and keep continuity of patt, starting at side seam, change to size 8 needles, knit across sts on stitch holder and then cont across rem sts. Cont in patt to armhole.

• **Armhole:** BO 8 (8, 8, 9, 9) sts at armhole edge, dec 1 st at armhole edge EOR 4 (4, 4, 5, 5) times—26 (30, 34, 34, 36) sts. Cont in patt until armhole measures 6¼ (6½, 6½, 6½, 7)".

• **Neck:** BO 10 (12, 12, 12, 12) sts at neck edge, dec 1 st at neck edge EOR 5 (5, 5, 5, 5) times— 11 (13, 17, 17, 19) sts. Cont until armhole measures 8 (8½, 9, 9½, 10)", ending on RS row.

• Beg short-row shaping on next WS row. Purl to 3 (4, 7, 7, 8) sts from end, W and T, knit back. Purl to 8 (9, 10, 10, 11) sts from end, W and T, knit back. Purl 1 row to retrieve wraps. Place sts on stitch holder.

Right Front

• With size 8 needles, CO 38 (42, 46, 48, 50) sts (includes 4 extra sts for front border). Knit 11 (11, 11, 13, 13) rows. Change to size 10 needles. Keeping center front 4 sts in garter st, work as for back to end of first garter st section.

• **Divide for pocket:** Cont in patt on first 28 (28, 30, 32, 32) sts for 30 rows of St st. Leave rem sts on a holder. Place sts on stitch holder. Working on last 10 (14, 16, 16, 18) sts only, CO 2 sts at inside edge of pocket and work the 30 rows of St st, on last row BO 2 sts at pocket edge. Place sts on stitch holder. Join 2 pieces tog: keep continuity of patt, change to size 8 needles, starting at center front, knit across sts on stitch holder, and then cont across rem sts. Cont in patt to armhole.

• Work armhole as for left front, reversing shaping.

• **Neck:** BO 10 (12, 12, 12, 12) sts at neck edge, dec 1 st at neck edge EOR 5 (5, 5, 5, 5) times— 11 (13, 17, 17, 19) sts. Cont until armhole measures 8 (8½, 9, 9½, 10)", ending on WS row.

• **Short-row shaping:** On next RS row, knit to 3 (4, 7, 7, 8) sts from end, W and T, purl back. Knit to 8 (9, 10, 10, 11) sts from end, W and T, purl back. Knit 1 row to retrieve wraps. Place sts on a holder.

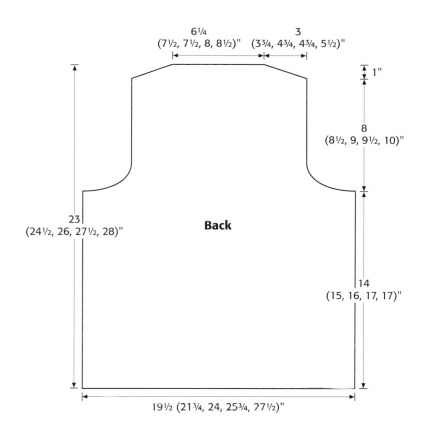

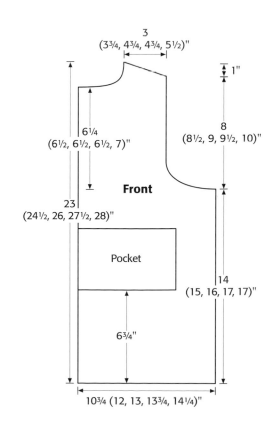

Finishing

- Work 3-needle BO for shoulders.

- **Collar:** With size 10 needles and WS facing, PU 10 (12, 12, 12, 12) sts across bound-off sts on neck edge, 10 (10, 11, 12, 14) sts to shoulder, 22 (26, 28, 28, 30) sts across back neck, 10 (10, 12, 12, 14) sts to shoulder, 10 (12, 12, 12, 12) sts across bound-off sts on neck edge—62 (70, 74, 76, 82) sts. **Row 1:** Knit. **Row 2:** K4, M1, knit to 4 sts from the end, M1, K4. Rep these 2 rows for 3 (3½, 3½, 4, 4)", ending with row 2. BO loosely.

- **Pockets:** With size 4 needles and 2 ply Shetland, PU 32 sts on inside flap of pocket with RS facing. Work in St st until pocket fits to front border. BO all sts, whipstitch pocket to inside of front.

- **Armhole bands:** With size 8 needles, starting at underarm seam, PU 8 (8, 8, 9, 9) sts across bound-off edge, 8 (8, 10, 10, 10) sts on dec edge, and 26 (28, 30, 32, 34) sts to shoulder, rep in reverse for other side, PM—84 (88, 96, 102, 106) sts. Working in the round, purl 1 round. CO 3 sts, work garter st I-cord as follows: *K2, SSK with last st CO and first st on left knitting needle. Sl the 3 sts as if to purl back to left needle, pull yarn tightly across the back, P2, P2tog with last st of I-cord and first st on left knitting needle.

Wyib, sl the 3 sts back to left needle as if to purl and rep from * around. BO.

- Weave side seams tog and tack down at underarm seam.

- **Zipper:** With crochet thread, overcast the front of the vest together, matching garter st ridges. Baste zipper in place on wrong side using contrasting sewing thread. Backstitch the zipper to the vest with matching sewing thread. Whipstitch the edge of the zipper tape to the knitting. If the zipper is too long, cut the excess off from the top of the zipper, leaving ½". Fold the ½" section to the underside of the zipper and tack down as zipper is sewn in. Remove crochet thread.

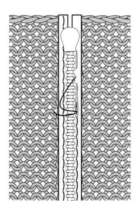

Backstitch zipper to wrong side.

Philadelphia

I couldn't believe my eyes when I saw this beautiful pattern form on the purl side simply because I worked a yarn over in various combinations with knit 2 together on the knit side of the vest. The pattern resembles a cable close up, but it isn't. This pattern is great for both men and women, and would be just as beautiful in one color.

Skill Level: Experienced

Sizes: Small (Medium, Large, X-Large, XX-Large)

Finished Chest: 36 (40, 44, 48, 52)"

Finished Length: 22 (23, 24, 24½, 25)"

Materials

Parfait Solids from Knit 1, Crochet 2 (100% pure worsted wool; 218 yds, 100 g per skein) in the following amounts and colors:

(MC) dark   2 (2, 3, 3, 4) skeins color 1292, or other worsted weight yarn

(A) medium 2 (2, 2, 2, 3) skeins color 1212, or other worsted weight yarn

(B) light   1 (1, 1, 1, 1) skein color 1244, or other worsted weight yarn

24" size 6 circular needles

24" size 8 circular needles (or size required to obtain gauge)

4 stitch holders

2 ring markers

1 safety pin

Gauge

18 sts and 24 rows = 4" in pattern stitch on size 8 needles

Ribbing Pattern

Row 1 (WS): (K1, P1) to last st, K1.

Row 2: (P1, K1) to last st, P1.

Pattern Stitch

Row 1 (WS): K11 (16, 20, 24, 29), *SSK, YO, K1, YO, K2tog, K1, SSK, YO, K1, YO, K2tog*, K14, SSK, YO, SSK, YO, K1, YO, K2tog, YO, K2tog, K14. Rep from * to * once, K11 (16, 20, 24, 29).

Row 2: Purl.

Rep rows 1 and 2.

Stripe Pattern

4 rows color A

2 rows color B

4 rows color A

10 rows MC

Cut yarn at the end of each section

Back

• With size 6 needles and MC, CO 75 (85, 93, 101, 111) sts. Work rib patt for 2 (2, 2½, 2½, 3)" ending with WS row. Knit next row, inc 6 sts evenly spaced across row   81 (91, 99, 107, 117) sts. Change to size 8 needles, beg patt st and stripe patt, and cont until piece measures 13 (14, 14½, 15, 15)".

• **Armhole:** BO 6 (7, 8, 8, 9) sts at beg of next 2 rows. Maintain patt st and stripe patt as established, dec 1 st at each end EOR 5 (6, 6, 7, 8) times—59 (65, 71, 77, 83) sts. Cont until armhole measures 8½ (8½, 9, 9, 9½)", ending on WS row.

• **Left shoulder:** Work across 15 (17, 19, 21, 23) sts, leave rem 44 (48, 52, 56, 60) sts on left needle, purl back, dec 1 st at neck edge on RS rows EOR twice. BO 13 (15, 17, 19, 21) shoulder sts.

• **Right shoulder:** Rejoin yarn at neck edge with RS facing, BO center 29 (31, 33, 35, 37) sts, cont across 15 (17, 19, 21, 23) sts. Dec 1 st at neck edge EOR twice on RS rows. BO 13 (15, 17, 19, 21) shoulder sts.

Front

Note: To work dec in patt at start of V neck, it may be necessary to leave out a YO next to a dec instead of working a traditional dec.

• Work as for back to armhole shaping. BO 6 (7, 8, 8, 9) sts at beg of next RS row, and *at same time* work V neck. Work across 34 (38, 41, 45, 49) sts, place center st on pin, drop off needle, turn, purl back.

• **Left front:** Dec 1 st at armhole edge EOR 5 (6, 6, 7, 8) times, *at same time* dec 1 st at neck edge EOR until 13 (15, 17, 19, 21) sts rem. When armhole measures 9 (9, 9½, 9½, 10)", BO all sts.

• **Right front:** Reattach yarn at center front with RS facing. Work as for left front, reversing shaping.

Finishing

• Weave shoulder seams and side seams tog.

• **Armhole bands:** With size 6 needles and MC, starting at underarm seam, PU 6 (7, 8, 8, 9) sts on bound-off edge, 40 (40, 44, 44, 48) sts to shoulder seam, rep in reverse for other side, PM—92 (94, 104, 104, 114) sts. Working in the round, purl 1 round. Work K1, P1 rib for 4 rounds. BO loosely in patt.

• **Neckband:** With size 6 needles and MC, starting at right shoulder seam, PU 35 (37, 39, 41, 43) sts to left shoulder seam, 41 (43, 45, 49, 51) sts to center front, PM, knit 1 st from pin, PU 41 (43, 45, 49, 51) sts to right shoulder seam, PM—118 (124, 130, 140, 146) sts. Working in the round, purl 1 round. Work in K1, P1 rib for 1 round. Always knit center st on pin. **Round 3:** Rib to 2 sts from center front, SSK, K1 on pin, K2tog, rib to end. **Round 4:** Rib to 2 sts before center, SSP, K1, P2tog, rib to end. Rep rounds 3 and 4 one more time. BO loosely in patt, working dec as for row 1 at center front.

• Mist with water and pin out to measurements. You can steam gently, but do not flatten the YO st patt.

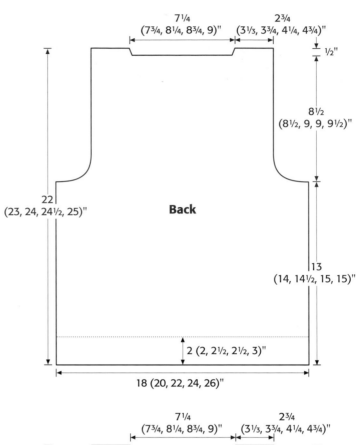

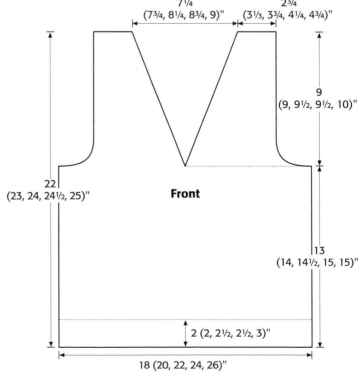

Lexington

Don't let the intarsia in this vest scare you. It's as simple as it gets. The chart is easy to read and there are very few ends to weave in when you're finished. Can't you picture the vest in bright colors for a woman?

Skill Level: Intermediate

Sizes: Small (Medium, Large, X-Large, XX-Large)

Finished Chest: 36 (40, 44, 48, 52)"

Finished Length: 22 (23½, 25, 26, 26½)"

Materials

Cascade 220 from Cascade Yarns (100% worsted wool; 220 yds, 100 g per skein) in the following amounts and colors:

(A)   2 (2, 3, 3, 4) skeins color 9341, or other worsted weight yarn

(B)   2 (2, 2, 2, 3) skeins color 9338, or other worsted weight yarn

(C)   1 (1, 1, 1, 1) skein color 4010, or other worsted weight yarn

24" size 5 circular needles

24" size 7 circular needles (or size required to obtain gauge)

4 stitch holders

1 ring marker

Sharp tapestry needle for weaving in ends from color work

Gauge

20 sts and 28 rows = 4" in stockinette stitch on size 7 needles

Back

• With size 5 needles and color A, CO 82 (92, 102, 112, 122) sts. Work ribbing for 2½ (3, 3, 3½, 3½)" as follows for all rows: K3, *P2, K2, rep from * to last 3 sts, end P3. On last WS row inc 8 sts evenly spaced across row—90 (100, 110, 120, 130) sts. Change to size 7 needles and cont in St st until piece measures 6 (6, 6, 6¼, 7)", ending on RS row.

• **Beg chart A:** Work to row 22, rep rows 21 and 22 until piece measures 10 (11, 12, 12, 13)".

• **Beg chart B:** Work to row 38, then rep rows 37 and 38 for remainder of vest. Cont in patt until piece measures 13 (14, 15, 15½, 16)".

• **Armholes:** BO 5 (7, 9, 10, 11) sts at beg of next 2 rows. Dec 1 st at each end EOR 4 (5, 6, 6, 6) times—72 (76, 80, 88, 96) sts. Cont until armhole measures 8 (8½, 9, 9½, 9½)".

• **Neck and right shoulder:** Work across 20 (22, 22, 25, 27) sts only. Keeping continuity of chart B, dec 1 st at neck edge EOR twice—18 (20, 20, 23, 25) sts. Beg short-row shaping on next WS row. Purl to 4 (6, 6, 7, 7) sts from end, W and T, knit back. Purl to 14 (14, 14, 16, 18) sts from end of row, W and T, knit back. Purl 1 more row to retrieve wraps. Place sts on stitch holder.

• **Neck and left shoulder:** Reattach yarn at neck edge with RS facing. BO 32 (32, 36, 38, 42) sts. Cont across 20 (22, 22, 25, 27) sts, keeping continuity of chart A. Dec 1 st at neck edge EOR twice—18 (20, 20, 23, 25) sts. Beg short-row shaping on next RS row. Knit to 4 (6, 6, 7, 7) sts from end, W and T, purl back. Knit to 14 (14, 14, 16, 18) sts from end of row, W and T, purl back. Knit one more row to retrieve wraps. Place sts on stitch holder.

Front

• Work as for back until piece measures 2½ (3½, 3½, 3½, 3½)" from start of armhole shaping, ending with WS row.

• **Left V neck and shoulder:** Keeping continuity of chart B, work across first 36 (38, 40, 44, 48) sts, leaving rem 36 (38, 40, 44, 48) sts on a holder or knitting needle. Dec 1 st at neck edge EOR 18 (18, 20, 21, 23) times, *at same time* when armhole measures 8 (8½, 9, 9½, 9½)", work short-row shaping as given for back right shoulder. Place rem 18 (20, 20, 23, 25) sts on a holder.

• **Right V neck and shoulder:** With RS facing, attach yarn at center front, keeping continuity of chart A, work dec as for left front V neck. Cont until armhole measures 8 (8½, 9, 9½, 9½)". Work short-row shaping as for back left shoulder. Place sts on stitch holder.

Finishing

• Work 3-needle BO for shoulders.

• Weave side seams tog.

• **Neckband:** With size 5 needles and B, starting at center front, CO 1 st, PU 34 (35, 38, 41, 41) sts to right shoulder seam, 48 (48, 52, 54, 58) sts across back neck, 34 (35, 38, 41, 41) sts to center front—117 (119, 129, 137, 141) sts. Turn, work (P2, K2) to last st, P1. Next 2 rows: **Row 1:** (RS) K1 (P2, K2). **Row 2:** (P2, K2) to end, P1. Rep rows 1 and 2 twice and then row 1 once more. BO all sts loosely. Overlap the edges of the band right over left. Whipstitch the left front band to the underside of the right front band to the seam allowance rem from picking up sts. Using the K1 on the edge of the right front band, weave it to the line on the left front where the sts were picked up for the bands.

• **Armbands:** With size 5 needles and MC, starting at underarm seam, PU 5 (7, 9, 10, 11) sts across bound-off sts, 41 (45, 47, 48, 49) sts to shoulder seam, rep in reverse for opposite side, PM— 92 (104, 112, 116, 120) sts. Working in the round, work in K2, P2 rib for 5 (5, 6, 6, 7) rows. BO all sts loosely.

• With sharp tapestry needle, weave in all ends from color work.

• Weave side seams together with blunt needle.

• Block gently by misting with water, pin out to correct measurements and then steam the garment with iron held about ½" above knitting. Do not allow the iron to touch the knitting. Smooth with hands. Keep flat until dry. Rep for other side.

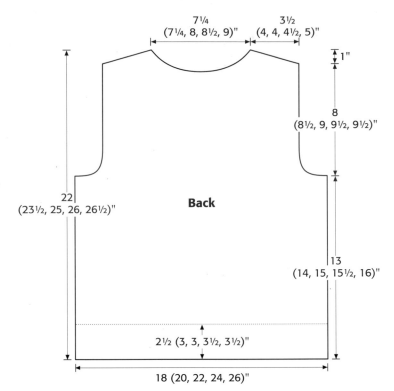

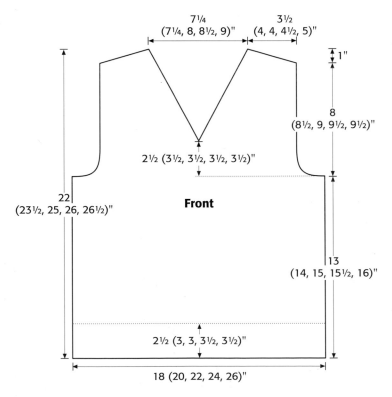

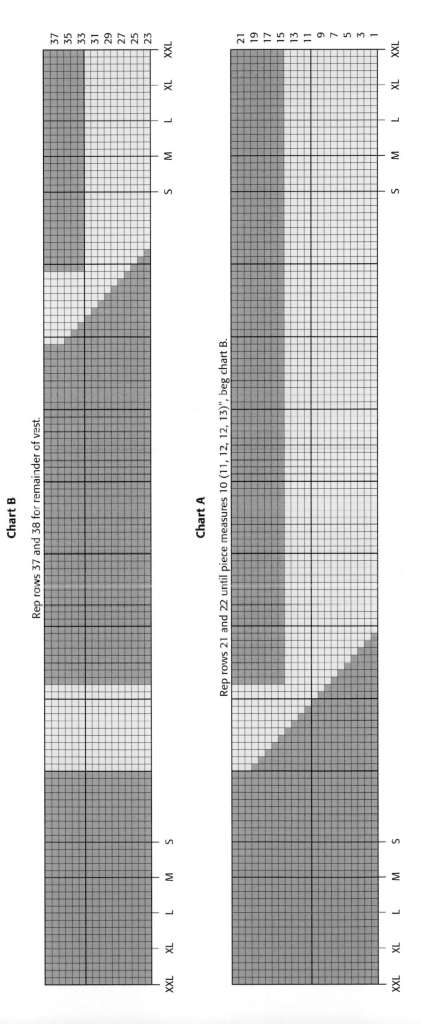

Chart B

Rep rows 37 and 38 for remainder of vest.

Chart A

Rep rows 21 and 22 until piece measures 10 (11, 12, 12, 13)", beg chart B.

Olympic Peninsula

Soft, yummy, alpaca and angora yarn mixed with a hematite bead make this gorgeous vest with lots of details. The shaping for the fronts are worked with some simple short rows. The bead knitting is simple and addictive. You won't be able to put it down. Several knitting needles are required for this vest, but it's worth it.

Skill Level: Experienced

Sizes: Small (Medium, Large, X-Large, XX-Large)

Finished Chest: 36 (39, 44, 48, 53)"

Finished Length: 21 (22, 22½, 24, 25)"

Materials

4 (4, 5, 5, 6) skeins Indulgence from Cascade Yarns (70% superfine alpaca and 30% angora; 246 yds, 100 g per skein) color 509, or other light worsted weight yarn

29" sizes 3, 4, and 7 circular needles (or size required to obtain gauge)

16" sizes 3 and 4 circular needles for armbands only

2 (2, 3, 4, 4) tubes of Hematite 6/0 seed beads, each tube weighing approx 1 oz/30 g (approximately 400 beads per tube)

Small amount of lightweight cotton yarn in a contrasting color for provisional cast on

Size G crochet hook

4 stitch holders

1 ring marker

1 sewing needle

8" of sewing thread in a contrasting color

Gauge

20 sts and 28 rows = 4" in stockinette stitch with beads on size 7 needles

How to Knit With Beads

To string the beads on the yarn, use a regular sewing needle with a piece of sewing thread about 8" long threaded through the eye of the needle and then folded over and the two ends knotted together. The sewing thread creates a large eye for the yarn to go through.

Do not thread more than 50 to 70 beads on the yarn at a time. The friction of the beads moving up and down on the yarn will ruin the surface of the yarn. When you run out of beads, you will have to cut the yarn and restring beads. Do this at an edge, not in the middle of the knitting.

To knit with beads, follow the chart for bead placement. Knit to the st where a bead is to be placed. Move a bead up to the knitting, knit into the back of the next st, pushing the bead through as you knit the st. On the return purl row, force the bead to sit on the knit side. Sometimes the beads want to slip to the space between two sts; you can use your fingers to push a bead back in position. Once the purl row is completed, the beads do not move as much.

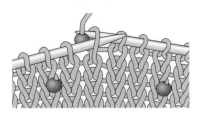

Knit into the back of the stitch, pushing the bead through as you knit.

Do not place a bead on the first or last st of a row. You don't want a bead in the seam or on the edge where sts are picked up.

Back

• *String about 70 beads on main yarn; set aside.

• **Provisional cast on for hem:** With the cotton yarn, crochet a loose chain of 90 (98, 110, 122, 134) sts. Finish off, cut yarn, and tie a knot in the end of the yarn so you know from which end to pull out the chain. Turn the chain over and with size 3 needle, and main yarn with beads, insert needle into loop on back of chain and knit on a st 9see page 49). Cont across until all sts are picked up for your size. Work in St st for 5 more rows, starting with a purl row.

Next row: K1, (YO, K2tog) across, K1. P1 row. Change to size 4 needle, K2, (K 1 bead into next st, K1) across. Work 5 more rows St st.

• **To create hem:** Unravel the crochet chain from the end with the knot in the tail, placing 1 st at a time on a size 3 needle. With RS facing, fold the hem sts on size 3 needle toward the back of the work and next to sts on size 4 needles. With size 7 needle, knit 1 st from front needle and 1 st from back needle tog* across the row (see page 49). Work in St st for 5 more rows. You may need to string on more beads here. Beg bead placement chart and cont until piece measures 12 (12½, 13, 14, 15)" from bottom of hem.

• **Armhole:** Keeping continuity of bead placement chart, BO 6 (7, 9, 9, 10) sts at beg of next 2 rows, BO 5 (4, 5, 6, 8) sts at beg of next 2 rows. Dec 1 st at each end EOR 3 (4, 4, 6, 6) times— 62 (68, 74, 80, 86) sts. Cont in patt until armhole measures 8 (8½, 8½, 9, 9)".

• **Back neck and right shoulder:** Work across 17 (19, 21, 23, 25) sts, leave rem 45 (49, 53, 57, 61) sts on large holder or knitting needle. Dec 1 st EOR twice at neck edge—15 (17, 19, 21, 23) sts, and *at same time* beg short-row shaping on next WS row. Purl to 5 (6, 7, 7, 8) sts from end, W and T, knit back. Purl to 10 (11, 12, 14, 15) sts from end of row, W and T, knit back. Purl 1 more row to retrieve wraps. Place sts on stitch holder.

• **Back neck and left shoulder:** Reattach yarn at neck edge with RS facing. BO 28 (30, 32, 34, 36) sts, cont across 17 (19, 21, 23, 25) sts. Dec 1 st EOR twice at neck edge, and *at same time* beg short-row shaping on next RS row. Knit to 5 (6, 7, 7, 8) sts from end, W and T, purl back. Knit to 10 (11, 12, 14, 15) sts from end of row, W and T, purl back. Knit one more row to retrieve wraps. Place sts on stitch holder.

Right Front

• ****Work from * to * of back,** except CO 46 (50, 56, 62, 68) sts. After hem is completed**, purl 1 row.

• **Beg right front chart for short rows and bead placement as follows:** Each "stair step" on the chart shows where a short row should be made. To start: **Rows 1 and 2:** K11, W and T, purl back. **Rows 3 and 4:** K15, (as you pass wrap from previous W and T, knit up that wrap), W and T, purl back. **Rows 5 and 6:** Place beads where shown, K19 (as you pass wrap from previous W and T, knit up that wrap), W and T, purl back. Proceed in this manner, following chart to row 17, where you will knit all the way across, placing beads only where shown. Work rows 18 through 29 and rep until piece measures 12 (12½, 13, 14, 15)" from bottom of hem.

• **Neck and armhole:** Dec 1 st at neck edge every fourth row 11 (11, 12, 12, 12) times, then EOR

6 (7, 7, 8, 9) times. *At same time* BO 6 (7, 9, 9, 10) sts for armhole at beg of first WS row, then BO 5 (4, 5, 6, 8) sts on next WS row. Dec 1 st EOR at armhole edge 3 (4, 4, 6, 6) times—15 (17, 19, 21, 23) sts. Cont until armhole measures 8 (8½, 8½, 9, 9)", ending on WS row.

• Work short rows as for back left shoulder. Place sts on stitch holder.

Left Front

• Work from ** to ** of right front.

• **Beg left front chart for short rows and bead placement as follows:** Rows 2 and 3: P11, W and T, knit back. **Rows 4 and 5:** P15, (as you pass wrap from previous W and T, purl up that wrap), W and T, knit back. **Rows 6 and 7:** P19 (as you pass wrap from previous W and T, purl up that wrap), W and T, knit back, place beads where shown. Proceed in this manner, following chart to Row 19, where you will knit all the way across, placing beads only where shown. Work rows 20 through 31 and rep until piece measures 12 (12½, 13, 14, 15)" from bottom of hem.

• Work armhole and neck shaping as for right front, reversing shaping.

• Work short rows as for back right shoulder. Place sts on stitch holder.

Finishing

• Work 3-needle BO for shoulders.

• Weave side seams tog.

• Weave hem tog at side seam, working the underside first and then the right side.

• **Armhole bands:** With beads threaded on yarn and 16" size 4 needle, starting at under-arm seam, PU 6 (7, 9, 9, 10) sts across first bound-off section, 4 (4, 5, 6, 8) sts across second bound-off section, 41 (41, 41, 43, 43) sts to shoulder seam, rep in reverse for other side, PM—102 (104, 110, 116, 122) sts. Working in the round, knit 4 rounds. **Next round:** (K2tog, knitting bead into sts, YO) around. Change to 16" size 3 needle. Knit 5 rounds. BO all sts. Loosely whipstitch the bound-off sts to the seam allowance left from picking up sts.

• **Neckband:** String 142 (147, 152, 162, 166) beads on yarn. (We have to break the rule for how many beads to string because you don't want to run out while knitting the band.) With 29" size 4 needle, starting at lower edge of right front, PU 80 (80, 84, 88, 92) sts to start of V neck, 42 (46, 46, 50, 50) sts to right shoulder seam, 40 (42, 44, 48, 48) sts to left shoulder seam, 42 (46, 46, 50, 50) sts to end of V neck, 80 (80, 84, 88, 92) sts to bottom of left front—284 (294, 304, 324, 332) sts. Work St st for 5 rows. **Next row:** (K2tog, knitting bead into sts, YO) around. Change to 29" size 3 needle, work St st for 5 rows. Loosely BO all sts. Loosely whipstitch the bound-off sts to the seam allowance left from picking up sts.

• Mist with water, lay flat to dry. Pin out to measurements. Gently steam with iron, but do not allow the iron to touch the knitting or the beads.

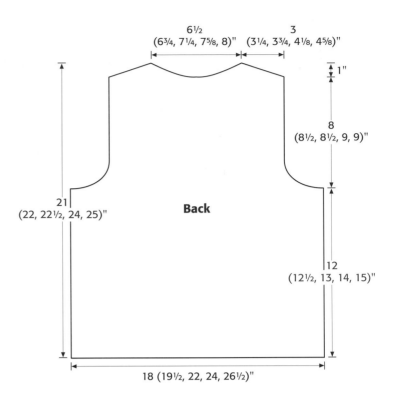

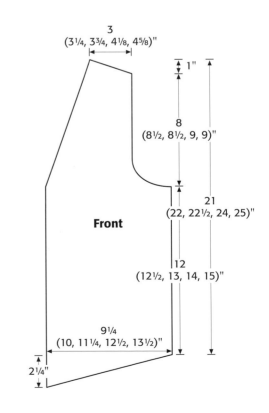

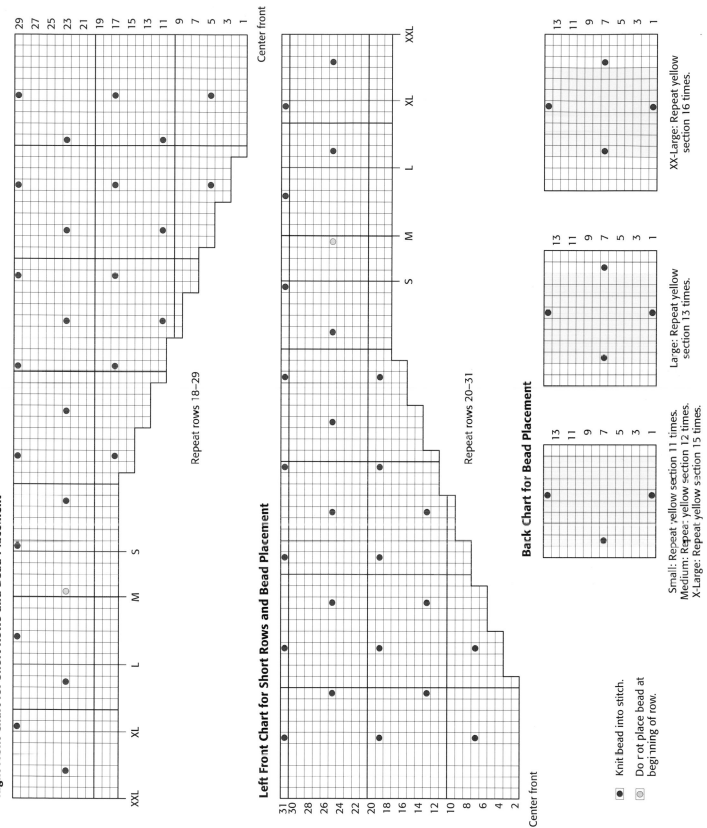

Right Front Chart for Short Rows and Bead Placement

Repeat rows 18–29

Center front

Left Front Chart for Short Rows and Bead Placement

Repeat rows 20–31

Center front

Back Chart for Bead Placement

XX-Large: Repeat yellow section 16 times.

Large: Repeat yellow section 13 times.

Small: Repeat yellow section 11 times.
Medium: Repeat yellow section 12 times.
X-Large: Repeat yellow section 15 times.

● Knit bead into stitch.

◉ Do not place bead at beginning of row.

Resources

Below is a list of the wonderful yarn companies that supplied the yarn for this book. As always I am in awe of their generosity and of the wonderful array of yarns that I get to choose from when I write a book. Thank you.

For a list of stores in your area that carry the yarns and beads mentioned in this book, contact the following companies.

YARNS

Berroco, Inc.
PO Box 367
Uxbridge, MA 01569-0367
www.berroco.com

Brown Sheep Yarns
100662 CR 16
Mitchell, NE 69357
www.brownsheep.com

Cascade Yarns
PO Box 58168
Tukwila, WA 98138-1168
www.cascadeyarns.com

Classic Elite Yarns
12 Perkins St.
Lowell, MA 01852

Dale of Norway, Inc
N16 W23390 Stoneridge Dr.,
Ste. A
Waukesha, WI 53188
www.dale.no

Knit One, Crochet Two
7 Commons Ave, Ste. 2
Windham, ME 04062
www.knitonecrochettoo.com

Harrisville Yarns
Harrisville Designs
PO Box 806
Harrisville, NH 03450
www.harrisville.com

Jamieson's Shetland Yarn
Unicorn Books
1338 Ross St.
Petaluma, CA 94954-1117

JCA/Reynolds Yarns
35 Scales Ln.
Townsend, MA 01469

Mountain Colors
PO Box 156
Corvallis, MT 59828
www.mountaincolors.com

Noro Yarns
Knitting Fever, Inc.
35 Debevoise Avenue
Roosevelt, NY 11575-0502
www.knittingfever.com

Rowan Yarns
Westminister Fibers, Inc
5 Northern Blvd. #3
Amherst, NH 03031-2230

Skacel Collection, Inc
PO Box 88110
Seattle, WA 98168
www.skacelknitting.com

Bibliography

S. R. Kertzer
105 A Winges Rd.
Woodbridge, ON L4L 6C2
Canada
www.kertzer.com

Tahki • Stacy Charles, Inc.
1059 Manhattan Ave.
Brooklyn, NY 11222
www.tahkistacycharles.com

Trendsetter Yarns
16745 Saticoy St.
Van Nuys, CA 91406

BEADS

Beyond Beadery
PO Box 460
Rollinsville, CO 80474
www.beyondbeadery.com

Wiseman, Nancie M. *Knitted Shawls, Stoles, and Scarves.* Woodinville, Wash.: Martingale and Company, 2001.

_____. *Knitted Sweaters for Every Season.* Woodinville, Wash.: Martingale and Company, 2002.

_____. *The Knitter's Book of Finishing Techniques.* Woodinville, Wash.: Martingale and Company, 2002.

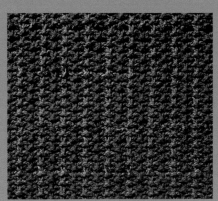
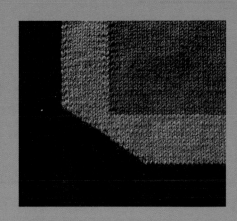

About the Author

While working as a registered nurse in 1987, Nancie opened a yarn shop, Nancie Knits, in Sacramento, California. While the store has long since closed, Nancie continues to teach classes locally and nationally, and to design and write knitting patterns and books for several companies, including Prism, Lorna's Laces, Rainbow Mills, Cascade Yarns, and Trendsetter Yarns. Her articles on knitting have been published in *Interweave Knits, Knit 'n Style*, and *Knitter's* magazines and an article on crochet appeared in a Fall 1999 *Piecework*. She has also published designs for *Knitters* and *Cast On Magazine*. In the fall of 1997, Nancie was the consultant for "Knitting 101," an article in *Martha Stewart Living*. Nancie's production company, Wisewater Productions, started in 1995, has produced seven bestselling videos to date. Nancie has recently added a new job to her knitting career. She will be a contributing editor to *Cast On Magazine* for The Knitting Guild of America.

Nancie's books include *Knitted Shawls, Stoles, and Scarves* (Martingale and Company, 2001), *Knitting for Every Season* (Martingale and Company, 2002), and *The Knitter's Guide to Knitting and Finishing Techniques* (Martingale and Company, 2002). This book, *Classic Knitted Vests*, is Nancie's sixth book, with a seventh book on the way.

Nancie lives on Whidbey Island, Washington, in the quaint town of Coupeville with her husband, Bill Attwater, and their dogs, Amber and Pumpkin.

new and bestselling titles from

Martingale® & COMPANY
America's Best-Loved Knitting Books®

That Patchwork Place®
America's Best-Loved Quilt Books®

NEW RELEASES
20 Decorated Baskets
Asian Elegance
Batiks and Beyond
Classic Knitted Vests
Clever Quilts Encore
Crocheted Socks!
Four Seasons of Quilts
Happy Endings
Judy Murrah's Jacket Jackpot
Knits for Children and Their Teddies
Loving Stitches
Meadowbrook Quilts
Once More around the Block
Pairing Up
Patchwork Memories
Pretty and Posh
Professional Machine Quilting
Purely Primitive
Shadow Appliqué
Snowflake Follies
Style at Large
Trashformations
World of Quilts, A

APPLIQUÉ
Appliquilt in the Cabin
Artful Album Quilts
Blossoms in Winter
Color-Blend Appliqué
Garden Party
Sunbonnet Sue All through the Year

HOLIDAY QUILTS & CRAFTS
Christmas Cats and Dogs
Christmas Delights
Creepy Crafty Halloween
Handcrafted Christmas, A
Hocus Pocus!
Make Room for Christmas Quilts
Snowman's Family Album Quilt, A
Welcome to the North Pole

LEARNING TO QUILT
101 Fabulous Rotary-Cut Quilts
Casual Quilter, The
Fat Quarter Quilts
More Fat Quarter Quilts
Quick Watercolor Quilts
Quilts from Aunt Amy
Simple Joys of Quilting, The
Your First Quilt Book (or it should be!)

PAPER PIECING
40 Bright and Bold Paper-Pieced Blocks
50 Fabulous Paper-Pieced Stars
Down in the Valley
Easy Machine Paper Piecing
For the Birds
It's Raining Cats and Dogs
Papers for Foundation Piecing
Quilter's Ark, A
Show Me How to Paper Piece
Traditional Quilts to Paper Piece

QUILTS FOR BABIES & CHILDREN
Easy Paper-Pieced Baby Quilts
Even More Quilts for Baby
More Quilts for Baby
Play Quilts
Quilts for Baby
Sweet and Simple Baby Quilts

ROTARY CUTTING/SPEED PIECING
101 Fabulous Rotary-Cut Quilts
365 Quilt Blocks a Year Perpetual Calendar
1000 Great Quilt Blocks
Around the Block Again
Around the Block with Judy Hopkins
Cutting Corners
Log Cabin Fever
Pairing Up
Strips and Strings
Triangle-Free Quilts
Triangle Tricks

SCRAP QUILTS
Nickel Quilts
Rich Traditions
Scrap Frenzy
Spectacular Scraps
Successful Scrap Quilts

TOPICS IN QUILTMAKING
Americana Quilts
Bed and Breakfast Quilts
Bright Quilts from Down Under
Creative Machine Stitching
Everyday Embellishments
Fabulous Quilts from Favorite Patterns
Folk Art Friends
Handprint Quilts
Just Can't Cut It!
Quilter's Home: Winter, The
Split-Diamond Dazzlers
Time to Quilt

CRAFTS
300 Papermaking Recipes
ABCs of Making Teddy Bears, The
Blissful Bath, The
Creating with Paint
Handcrafted Frames
Handcrafted Garden Accents
Painted Whimsies
Pretty and Posh
Sassy Cats
Stamp in Color

KNITTING & CROCHET
365 Knitting Stitches a Year
   Perpetual Calendar
Basically Brilliant Knits
Crochet for Tots
Crocheted Aran Sweaters
Knitted Sweaters for Every Season
Knitted Throws and More
Knitter's Template, A
Knitting with Novelty Yarns
More Paintbox Knits
Simply Beautiful Sweaters for Men
Today's Crochet
Too Cute! Cotton Knits for Toddlers
Treasury of Rowan Knits, A
Ultimate Knitter's Guide, The

8/03/K